Hazel Ett[illegible]ge

BEYOND WORDS

Journaling for Creativity and Clarity

Hedge Publishing

Beyond Words

Journaling for Creativity and Clarity

There is a story from the Zen Buddhist tradition about a monk who tried to show a friend the moon by pointing to it. For a long while the friend gazed upon the pointing finger but it was only when she looked beyond the finger, at the direction in which it pointed, that she saw the glory of the shining moon.

The journaling prompts in this book are like pointing fingers, guiding the direction of our gaze beyond the words that we write, towards a richer, deeper and more profound mystery that we might call our life.

Beyond Words

Hazel Ettridge

ISBN: 978-1-3999-2059-9

Published by Hedge Publishing. This book is produced entirely in the UK, is available to order from most book shops in the United Kingdom and is globally available via UK-based Internet book retailers and www.amazon.com.

The text pages of this book are produced via an independent certification process that ensures the trees from which the paper is produced come from well managed sources that exclude the risk of using illegally logged timber while leaving options to use post-consumer recycled paper as well.

Contents

Introduction

We all have a world view - what we think, what we believe, our values, our perspective on life, death and the universe in any given moment. Some of us may have maintained the same world view over a long period of time. For others, this view may change with our mood and circumstance or with the advent of new information or evidence. The creative prompts in this book are designed to playfully wriggle through our fixed ideas, to provoke or challenge or maybe to re-inforce our perspective on the world and our place in it. Using these prompts will invite clarity and a sense of wellbeing that comes from seeing and being seen more fully.

Each creative activity invites us to reach out, from a part that is foundational into a part that is in flux and growing. Like an octopus with a hundred tentacles, we can play and experiment. We can make our ordinary selves extraordinary and allow our extraordinary selves to be ordinary.

The journaling prompts have been loosely organised into sections and I encourage you to delve into them with a pick'n'mix approach. Treat each section like a course on a menu and, just as you wouldn't eat all the starters in one go, dip into the various sections as your fancy takes you.

We begin with 101 creative activities. Each activity starts with time limited **free writing**. This is a chance to warm up. To move from the left brain into the right brain – where creativity and clarity have space to show up. Free writing is a non-stop flow of words onto the page – don't think about it too much. If you hit a block, just keep repeating the last word or phrase that you wrote until another word arrives or you get to the end of your time. Grammar and punctuation have no place in this activity and there is no getting it right or wrong.

Free writing is followed by a **writing** prompt and suggestions for **making** something (usually artwork of some kind) and for physically **doing** something. It is entirely up to you whether you engage with all four aspects of the activity or choose just one or two. My recommendation, however, is that you try to get a mix. Writing may stimulate the mind's wisdom. Art may encourage the heart's clarity. Doing may engage the body in action – manifesting your creativity in the world.

Following on from the 101 activities, there is a template outlining a creative retreat. This is one that I created for myself, you might like to follow my schedule or use it as a springboard for designing your own retreat. The final prompt is a description of the Creative Weave technique from which you will be able to create many more journaling activities that will reflect your own interests and style. Last of all, is a section entitled Reflections. This is a long list of quotes and questions that can be used for quick fire inspiration and contemplation.

Creative journaling techniques cover everything from morning pages to daily haikus; from reflective writing to scribbling doodles while listening to poetry; from collecting wonderful images and metaphors that come into your head during long walks in nature to capturing fragments of dreams when you wake up in the morning. Your journal might include endless lists, mind maps, mandalas, unsent letters, diagrams, vision boards, poems, collages, little drawings and paintings, photographs, memories, reminders, affirmations, beautiful questions to sit with and more. These are all just tools in your tool box – if you decide that you want to break things apart or put them back together with your bare hands, then go ahead. Your journal is exactly that – YOURS. Work with it in whatever way you choose.

Allow yourself to approach journaling with the same appetite with which you might approach a good meal. As you pick up your pen and journal notebook, you might get that same sense of anticipation that precedes sitting down at the table to tuck in to some flavoursome food. The experience of journaling can be wonderfully stimulating to the 'taste buds' of the heart-mind and it will leave you feeling nourished and satisfied.

I hope these ideas will provoke clear and insightful thinking while delivering plenty of surprises. Each creative activity is an invitation – not an instruction. Please use them in a flexible way that suits your interests and resources. I would encourage you, while stretching beyond your comfort zone, not to push yourself into areas that might reinforce old or unhelpful patterns. Journaling can be incredibly therapeutic but it is not therapy. The landscape of your journal will be filled with both shadow and light – but no jumping off precipices, please!

Where've You Been All This Time?

If I died tomorrow, I'd be disappointed – because I still don't feel that I've lived a proper life. You know, the one I was supposed to live. Kurt Vonnegut talks about the trajectories of various story lines – from myths and fairy tales to contemporary novels, movies and TV dramas. No matter where the story begins on the scale of Good Fortune or Ill Fortune, he claims, our protagonist always begins by gaining a vision of happiness, an object of desire, a way to a better place – they move towards this beckoning future either through their own efforts (kindness, purity, intelligence, skill, hard work) or through external intervention (a fairy godmother, guardian angel, fate) only to have it all snatched away when catastrophe explodes onto the scene (wicked queens, ugly sisters, evil spells). But then comes redemption or rescue and the happy ever after is inevitable. On some level, I've been conditioned to expect my own life to follow this template, but ....real life is not often so clear cut.

Strangely, one of the happiest times of my life was when I had cancer. During that period, my friends and family all told me how much they loved me. Things that were close to my heart came to the fore and I gained a lot of clarity around the components of my life that I valued and those that I would be happy to let go of. Conversely, the worst period of my life was when I finally found myself at the top of my chosen career ladder - the stress was unbearable. I allowed myself to be starved of the things that nurtured and nourished me because I no longer had time for family or friends or for long walks in the woods. When I wasn't working, I wasn't fit for anything. It's a story I'm sure many of us can relate to.

The creative prompts in this section inquire into the story of your life so far.

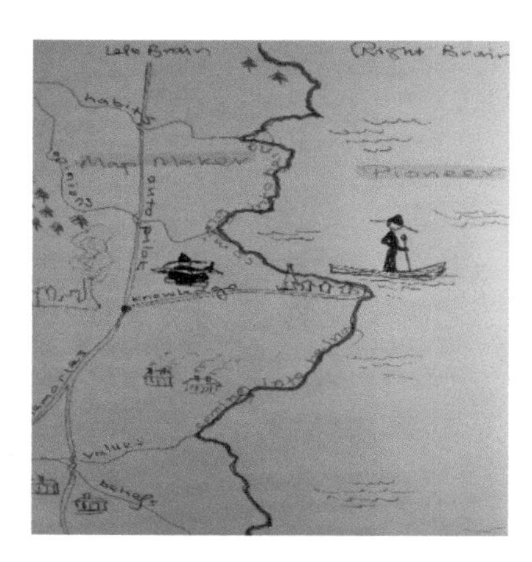

1. I love my stuff!

Looking at your life, a part-lived trajectory – where is the gold? What can you retrieve that will serve you today? What can you be grateful for? What help and support was always there – often unnoticed by your otherwise-engaged self?

Free writing (3 minutes)

- Sitting comfortably, take a wander through your body, notice sensations and relax where you can. Imagine that you are slipping, very slowly into a warm pool of water, feeling it gently lulling you into a sense of wellbeing. As you relax, call to mind a treasured belonging (it could be a current possession or something from the past). Ponder for a moment – what does it mean to 'belong'? To be in a state of longing?

Write

- Try writing from the point of view of that possession (in the first person) - it's probably best if it is an inanimate object. Write how 'you' feel, something of 'your' history, any aspirations 'you' may have - anything that comes to mind. It can be interesting and freeing to write with your non-dominant hand.

I am a kaleidoscope. I am a thing of beauty and fascination. I have been cleverly constructed and my workings are complex but my purpose in life is to bring pleasure, surprise and a sense that there is something of wonder beyond our normal mundane lives .... as she gazes into my aperture, she sees heaven – the universe – a storm of ever changing beauty and colour – she is reminded of her own true nature.'

Make

- Take a photo of the beloved possession. If it is no longer available to you, create an image that symbolises how you feel about it.

Do

- Look around the environment you find yourself in right now. Are there objects that you love or have loved? Do you overlook them on a daily basis? Have they become invisible to you? Become aware of how these objects can light a little flame in your heart as you notice them.

2. Tracks of my years

Making autobiographical lists can be interesting and illuminating. What do you include? What do you choose to omit?

Free writing (3 minutes)

- Scan through your life for music that has meant something to you. Or think of music that you absolutely love – a playlist for your funeral or for when you're down or for when you just want to dance or sing along.

Write

- Compile a list of tracks for a CD of your life. Scan through the years chronologically from your earliest memories. Allow your sense of nostalgia to play out.
- Use one of your tracks to start a piece of writing........ *Ruby Tuesday was lost and alone. She no longer tried to fit in. Her perspective on life was unique beyond words ...*
- Think of your list of tracks as chapter headings in your autobiography. Write a brief summary under each heading. Expand on a memory that calls to you.

Make

- Try to find an image (or several images) from a magazine or similar, that would make a good cover for your CD and stick or collage it on to a CD sized square of card or stiff paper. Cut out words for a catchy title. List your tracks on the reverse side of the card.

Do

- Play some of these tracks while you work.

Alternatively – instead of an autobiographical list, you could apply these journaling activities to a theme that is important to you, for example, a CD addressing climate change or mental wellbeing or addiction.

3. Food glorious food!

Music is a great theme for an autobiographical list – but so are many other things. I was thinking about the various foods that have accompanied me through different periods of my life.

Remembering back to childhood where most meals came from tins or packets. Sunday tea was always tinned fruit cocktail with condensed milk. Saturday was Angel Delight to finish off the fish and chip lunch. My mum and dad both worked, so I was left to look after my little sister in the school holidays and I was taught how to cook three hot dinners: tinned chicken soup, tinned tomato soup and Fray Bentos steak pie in a tin! I had to pierce the lid then sit the whole thing in a pan of simmering water for 30 minutes before using a can opener to remove the lid and reveal the soggy puff pastry and meaty gravy inside. I thought at the time (I was 7 or 8 years old) that I was a very accomplished cook. Over the years I've enjoyed many different cuisines - partly following trends (remember fondue?) and partly from visiting and living in other countries. I've been a vegetarian since leaving home in 1972 and am now vegan, enjoying very simple meals. Food has, at times, just been fuel to keep my body going and, at other times, it has been the most beautiful gift that I could give to myself and others.

Free writing (3 minutes)

- Indulge yourself in memories of foods you have loved and loathed. Mentally wander through your life noting the foods that came and went, and also the foods that have remained a constant joy (roast potatoes and gravy – yum!).

Write

- Make a list, by decade, of the foods that were prominent. What were your comfort foods? What foods did you find disgusting? Have you ever been on a diet? When were you introduced to new or interesting foods?

- Write about your relationship with food today. Do you cook with or for others? Do you bake with the children? Do you eat out? Takeaways? Picnics? Do you grow your own? Buy organic or local? Are there any changes you would like to make in the way you buy or prepare food?

Make

- Create a personal recipe book that captures your life – the kind of book you wish a much loved relative had left for you.
- Produce a gastronomic autobiographical collage using pictures from magazines.

Do

- Prepare a dish from your past to enjoy this week.

4. Windows on the World

Today we have so many windows on the world – TV and radio, books, newspapers and magazines, YouTube, Facebook, Instagram, TED talks, documentaries, films and endless zoom meetings, blogs and podcasts.....

When I was a child, my windows on the world were far more limited but still had great impact. The first film that opened my eyes to other realities was The Boy with Green Hair - made in 1948, about Peter, a war orphan, who was fostered by a family friend, Gramp. Problems arise when, one day, Peter's hair turns green. This gets a bad reaction from the villagers who try to force him to shave it off. I remember watching this film alone and there was a thunder storm going on outside (yes, really). I ended up hiding in a tiny space between the back of the sofa and the wall, waiting for my parents to come home. I must have been 5 or 6 years old. My horror (to the point of feeling nauseous) was for the boy whose 'difference' triggered such a negative response from the local community who seemed to think that they had the right to force him to conform. Even at that young age, I was learning the horror of prejudice and bigotry. Even though I didn't have the language to express it - I felt it in every bone.

Free writing (3 minutes)

- What is the first film you can remember watching? What effect did it have on you? On your view of the world?

Write

- Write a dialogue between your younger self (who watched the film) and your present-day self. Discuss the film and your responses to it.

Make

- While thinking about the film, allow yourself to feel the emotions it brings up. Close your eyes while doing so, let yourself doodle on a blank page. When you're ready, open your eyes and complete the doodle in any way you wish (add words, colours, further images, highlights, collaged images, textures).

Do

- Review your current Windows on the World. Reflect on how you look through these windows and on what you see. Are you drawn only to windows that re-affirm your current world view or are you interested in considering new truths?
- Think of a global theme that interests you. Find one new window on the world that relates to that theme and look through it.

5. Fragments of history

My home is FULL of stuff. Recently I've been noticing items, objects, utensils, art work that I haven't properly looked at or used for years. Things that sit on shelves, on the wall, at the back of cupboards.

I have candlesticks from my first marital home, bought in 1975. I've got a sugar bowl and milk jug from my grandma's china cabinet. I've got jewellery given to me by long ago lovers. I've got items brought back from my travels. Each one of these items is a treasure to feast on.

Free writing (3 minutes)

- Gather some memories of items from your past and let them tell you stories long forgotten.

Write

- Write a list of treasured items (or a poem or a list that is a poem).
- Dialogue with one of your treasures (it may have an interesting perspective on your past).
- Tell the story of how you came by this treasure – let it remind you of who you have been and who you have become.

Make

- Arrange your treasures as a still life and take a photograph – or take several photographs and make an album.

Do

- Use one of the items that has not been used for a while.
- Clean, polish and nurture your treasures.
- Display them in a new way or choose to give them away as valued gifts.
- Curate some of your treasures into a collection.

6. Beautiful Ruins

The poet David Whyte writes, 'Human ideas and human endeavour find their fullest form only as a beautiful ruin .... things find their full beauty only in the wear and tear of weather ......'. It seems to me that the edifices we try to build in our lives are only the packaging – packaging that often hides the gift within, but in the end, these edifices will be worn away, they will decay and disappear, leaving only the beautiful ruin of that gift.

Free writing (3 minutes)

- Leap into the future and imagine that it is 100 years since the day you were born - what do you think people might remember about you? What words, images, actions?

Write

- Try writing about the 'packaging' of your life – the career you built, the home you created, the lifestyle you took on, the self you presented to the world, the plans you made, the dreams you chased.

- Write about the gift within the packaging. The beautiful ruin that remains when all else is gone. The things that truly catch your heart's attention, the foundation of all your dreams and longings. Can you sum this up in a short phrase or perhaps a Haiku.

(A Haiku is usually a three line verse structured as 5 syllables/7 syllables/5 syllables.)

If you find it uncomfortable to write about yourself, write about someone you care for – describing the impact they make or have left behind.

Make

- Create a collaged mind map. Put yourself in the middle with lines extending out to represent different areas of your life where you have influenced or impacted the world and other people. Use images as well as words for each area – either torn from magazines or you can draw them yourself. Try to use bigger images where you feel you have made a greater impact.
- Alternatively – create a collaged mind map showing one specific area of your life, for example, how your carbon footprint has changed over the years and the ways in which it will continue to change in the future.

Do

- Visit an actual ruin. An historic building or an archaeological site. Imagine this place when it was newly built. Is the essence of its beauty still apparent? Perhaps it is even more beautiful in its ruined state.

7. Unhinged

A dear friend was talking the other day about viewing hinges as a symbol for what we allow to come into or be released from our lives. Hinges are a movable joint or mechanism on which a door (or a life) swings to allow the door (or life) to open and close. Without this flexible little gadget, a door (or a life) would be pretty stuck and useless. The word 'hinge' is also used to describe something that facilitates our decisions, for example, "it all hinges on the weather". So, it might be pretty useful to discover our own personal hinge and how we can keep it well oiled.

During the lockdowns of 2020 and 2021 many of us may have felt unhinged from our 'normal' lives and the way we have operated in the world up until now. The dictionary definition of unhinged states: 'to make unstable, unsettled, to disrupt and confuse'.

For me, my hinges get rusty and the door gets stuck when I am small minded, judgemental and living on autopilot. Keeping my hinges in good order involves being alert and aware of what my door is open to and what it is closed to – allowing me to remain open, kind, appreciative while at the same time maintaining boundaries that keep me safe and protected.

Free writing (3 minutes)

- When have you been lifted out of your normal routines - forcibly 'unhinged'? How do you re-hang your door? Do you need to re-position your door? In what ways does your hinge become rusty and stuck? How can you keep it well oiled?

Write

- Write about a time when you felt unhinged. What was happening? How did you feel? How did you resolve the situation? What personal qualities or beliefs might cause your hinges to rust or break?
- List some creative practices that might help to oil your hinges.

Make

- Make a reminder to oil your hinges. This could be a book mark, a cartoon, a drawing or painting, a post-it note stuck on the fridge door or a regular walk in nature. Finding ways to connect with mother earth is a wonderful way to oil your hinges.

Do

- Create a playlist of music that will oil your hinges when you're feeling rusty. Music that will loosen you up and make you feel good about yourself and your life. Music to dance to. Music to sing along with.

8. Bella and the Rat

My 12 year old cat has suddenly become a hunter. After the blue tit earlier in the week, yesterday she brought home a rat - maimed but still alive. She brought it to the back door and was giving it that one-pointed attention that only hunting cats can give - obviously pleased with herself for acting on her natural instincts, but having not much of a clue as to what she was supposed to do next. I scooped her up and into the house (much to her chagrin), and poked the rat, who ambled off into the undergrowth. Bella and I spent the rest of the day indoors.

It got me to thinking about all of the rats that I have hunted in my life – career success, money in the bank, designer shoes, an evening of opera at Glyndebourne, a trip to see the Aurora Borealis, the search for the ultimate chocolate cake, 5 minutes of fame on the TV, true love, a cottage in the country, a 20 year old single malt .... and most days I wake up looking for yet another rat to chase. But what do I do when I catch them? Just like Bella, I sit with a feeling that I should know what to do next - but I don't.

I exceeded my own expectations in my chosen career - so what? Nobody applauded. The designer clothes remain at the back of my wardrobe as I parade around in my beloved jeans. The 5 minutes of fame on TV went totally unnoticed by absolutely anyone. As I've grown older, my interest in rats has declined - I've learned that rats don't satisfy my appetite.

Free writing (3 minutes)

- List the rats in your life. Do they satisfy your hunger? If not, what might be a more satisfying meal?

Write

- Write a day (or even 5 minutes) in the life of one of your rats – write it in the first person from the perspective of the rat.

Make

- Create a triptych collage showing (1) the 'rats' you have chased in the past, (2) the 'rats' you think you should still be chasing and (3) the alternative meal that might be ultimately far more fulfilling.

Do

- Go hunting for a tasty titbit today. Relish the chase. Relish the meal.

9. Before We Go

A dear friend has set up a YouTube channel for 2 minute video posts where people can share any wisdom they have gleaned from life and that they feel might be worth putting out there. I am filled with gratitude for the words that people have chosen to share. (YouTube: Before We Go Michael Maynard)

Free writing (3 minutes)

- Let your mind roam freely through your history. Remember the people who shared their wisdom with you. Think about the situations and experiences that shaped and transformed your life. Reflect on the modest trail of understanding and the lightning Eureka strikes that formed your current insights into how and why you are here.

Write

- Write a letter to a younger person – perhaps someone in your family, or even to a younger self. What insights might you have to offer? What cautionary tales?

Make

- Create a collage bringing together all of the things you have found valuable in life.

Do

- If you have the technology, you might like to make a video and submit it to Michael's YouTube channel.

10. Your one, wild, precious life

The word 'church' comes from the Greek word ecclesia, meaning 'a called out company or assembly'. From this original idea of a gathering of people, these days it is more commonly used to describe a building or place of Christian worship.

Free writing (I suggest no more than a minute on each point)

Respond to the following questions:

- Where is your church? The woods or perhaps the beach? Maybe the cushion where you meditate in front of your little altar or the seat in the garden where you sit with your coffee, the cat on your lap listening to the birds singing? Or perhaps in front of the TV, at the theatre or cinema or the pub? The internet with its TED talks and Vimeo and YouTube?
- Which gods do you serve? The big supermarkets, tourism, the fashion industry, social media, Bacchus, Eros, Gaia? What is important in your life? What would it break your heart to lose - what can you not live without?
- How do you worship? Sitting quietly in nature? Queueing outside the supermarket? Spending hours online? Being with people who matter to you? Reading? Listening to music? Swimming in the sea? Activism for a cause you believe in? Volunteering time, energy, money? Obsessively cleaning the house or pruning the roses?
- What prayers do you say? What support do you long for - personally, for others and for the world? What are you grateful for? What do you love?
- Is there a community or assembly that speaks to your heart?

This is an opportunity to review and to crystallise how we bring meaning to our lives. As Mary Oliver says in her poem The Summer Day, 'Tell me, what is it you plan to do with your one wild precious life?'

Write

- Use your reflections as a spring board for a poem or a prayer or a letter to self.

Make

- Create a collage or painting that is a visual description of how your spirit moves in this world. Use colours, graphics, symbols, stick men, pictures cut from magazines, little drawings as well as words.

Do

- Perform one act of meaningful worship today.

11. I want to be 'us' not 'them'

Prejudice is a difficult thing to write about and apologies, but this is only a very light dressing on a very deep wound. I think our prejudices drive much of our thinking and many of our decisions and it's important that we make some effort to become more aware of them if we can bear it. The word prejudice is defined as an adverse judgement or a pre-conceived opinion that is not based on reason or experience - and it can lead to discrimination (the prejudicial treatment of an individual based on their membership of a certain group or category).

Free writing (3 minutes)

- It is interesting to think about the ways in which we are 'other'. We all want to be 'us' and not 'them'. But all of us have experienced being 'othered' at some point in our lives - for our gender, our sexuality, our dis-abilities, our religious views, our lifestyle, our cultural beliefs, our political views, our intelligence, our race, our mental health, our eccentricity, our honesty ... Is it possible to have some curiosity about this? When we disown other people, do we disown part of ourselves?

Write

- Write a reflective piece on the ways in which you are 'other'. Include the negative aspects (feeling rejected, unseen, misunderstood or under suspicion) and the positive aspects (feeling unique, special, proud).
- Now make a list of who you 'other'. Are there types of people you push away saying, "That is not me/my kind of person"?
- Choose someone that you 'other' and introduce them as the protagonist in a short story or piece of flash fiction. Write in the first person.

Make

- Draw an outline of yourself and fill it with words, colours, torn up bits of magazines, scraps of fabric to represent the parts of you that are 'one of us' and the parts of you that may be perceived as being 'one of them'.

Do

- Let one of your 'othered' parts come out to play. Take care of that part today. Nurture it. Pamper it.

12. Order and Chaos

I recently watched an interview with Iain McGilchrist. He speaks in such an interesting way about the functions of the right and left hemispheres of the brain.

Right brain: big picture, exploring possibilities, comfortable with chaos, like a wild garden, can live with anomalies and will use imagination to see how they might fit.

Left brain: beaurocrat, an emissary for the right brain, grasping and controlling, looking for certainty, a walled garden, blocks out anomalies - if it doesn't fit my view then it doesn't exist.

He suggests that living on the border between order and chaos is a very good idea if you want to live a full and interesting life. "Encounter as much uncertainty as you can tolerate". His definition of God is "a coming into being". So the God of the left hemisphere is fixed (as in many religions) and the God of the right hemisphere is in a constant process of coming into being - through living things (like us!).

As I listened to the interview an image came to mind - left brain as mapmaker and right brain as pioneer, each reliant on the other and (on a good day) both working together.

Free Writing (3 minutes)

- Where is your inner pioneer setting his/her sights? Are there roads that you are contemplating wandering down, sights you hope to see, ocean depths you want to explore, precipices on which you teeter? What's on your horizon? Is it possible to face the future with a willingness to "encounter as much uncertainly as you can tolerate"?

Write

- Chronicle one road on the map of your history. For example: From education to work. From family to independence. From faith to despair (or the other way around). From amateur to professional. From knowing the way to feeling lost.

Make

- Make a map showing the life you have already lived. Include cross roads, resting places, tough terrain and places of respite. The well known territories, the well travelled roads.

Do

- How will you extend your map today? Where does your pioneer wish to go? If this really is the first day of the rest of your life, what direction is calling? Take that first step.

13. Magic Things

There's a lovely quote from WB Yeats, "The world is full of magic things, patiently waiting for our senses to grow sharper."

Free Writing (3 minutes)

- Lockdown was a time to slow-down, an opportunity for our 'senses to grow sharper' resulting in our noticing that 'the world is full of magic things'. Walking in the woods, being mesmerised by birdsong or the light falling through the leaves. In what situations do your senses grow sharper?

Write

- Write a poem about your senses – vision, hearing, smell, taste, touch – perhaps one line for each sense. Let your senses grow sharper as you write. Feel the weight, density, smoothness, temperature of your pen. Marvel at the vision of ink as it appears on the page. Try writing with your non-dominant hand to enhance the awareness of forming letters.

Make

- Create something sensual – something that really speaks to your senses. A textured collage. A piece of embroidery or knitting. Bake aromatic biscuits. Go on a photo shoot and create an album of 'magic things'.

Do

- Next time you go for a walk, sharpen your senses - you might like to concentrate on just sound, vision or touch - or be fully sensual. Focus on receiving the outside world through your senses. Then, focus on your inner landscape.
- Next time you sit down to a meal, sharpen your sense of smell and taste to appreciate the magical qualities of flavour and nourishment.
- Right now, in this moment, what magic things are patiently waiting for your senses to grow sharper?

14. In the end you won't be known

I've often marvelled at the creativity and skill of cake decorators, who seem to have the artistry of great sculptors and yet their creations last for only a few days at most and are then eaten and lost forever. Like the work of artists who sculpt sand on a beach, or arrange stones in a landscape – it is the creative act that seems to matter, not the commoditising of the end result. I look at my life and see how much I want it to solidify, to become something that I can show to people and say, "Is that okay? Am I doing it right?"

In her poem, 'In the End' Tara Mohr says, "...in the end you won't be known. You won't be asked, by a vast creator full of light, what did you do to be known? You'll be asked: Did you know it, this place, this journey?....... You are here to pay attention. That is enough. In the End."

It's a great perspective shifting poem that takes all the pressure off building a showcase of a life and encourages us to live each day fully just as it comes.

Free Writing (3 minutes)

- Reflecting on the structures you have created in your life (cakes, sandcastles, careers...) – how many of them are still standing? How many of them are you still trying to prop up?

Write

- Write a sales pitch that showcases you and the life you have lived so far. Mention all of your achievements and successes – these might be in your own terms or in the terms of the society in which you live.

Make

- Create a mandala that encompasses the excitement, the trepidation, the eagerness and the reluctance, the warmth, the texture, the aliveness, the brightness, the colours, the flavours – what Tara Mohr calls 'the take-me-now-ness' that is your life.

Do

- Do something today that nobody else will know about – perhaps a small act of kindness.

15. The Story Book of Me

Our history is literally that – his/her story. Reality flows into, up against, through and around us all the time – how we deal with it and make sense of it becomes our story. Much of the pain in our lives emanates from the disconnection between our stories and what is happening in reality. So, it can be very useful to become aware of the stories in which we abide – the stories we are telling ourselves as we engage with life in the raw.

Free writing (3 minutes)

- Think about a time when you felt strong emotion. What story were you telling yourself in that moment? Some examples:

  - This is my happily ever after.
  - It's all his fault – he's so selfish.
  - What's the point – everyone just dies in the end.
  - I'm different – there's something fundamentally wrong with me.
  - If only I'm good enough then good things will happen to me.
  - Everyone else is so sorted. What's wrong with me?
  - When I've got this/done this/been there my life will be complete.
  - No-one will ever understand what I've been through.
  - This is so great – but it won't last.

Write

- Choose one of your stories and produce a synopsis (use the third person) for a short story.
- Consider writing The Story Book of Me - a fictional autobiography that tells it just the way you want it.

Make

- Create The Story Book of Me as a picture book. You could use images from magazines or actual photos.

Do

- Try out a different story today. Spend some time imagining that you are someone else – perhaps a role model or a favourite fictional character. How would they see this situation? How would they act in this scenario? What story would they be telling themselves?

Who Do You Think You Are?

I have asked myself this question so many times, and each time I've come up with a different answer. Hardly surprising when you think about the ever changing conversations we are having with the world and our lives as they emerge. Recently I've boiled my answer down to this: I am part Habit and part Potential. That's it. Part of me is what I've already been up until now and that I keep on repeating out of habit – thoughts, emotions, beliefs, ways of doing things. The other part of me is that which I don't yet know – but it is very real. It is my potential. Within these two parts there are so many stories and narratives to explore and to endure and to enjoy. That is what I have endeavoured to do with these invitations.

16. I am not a noun (I'm a verb)

This notion comes from the wonderful Braiding Sweetgrass by Robin Wall Kimmerer, who suggests that when we name something we fix it. By giving people, animals, features a label we categorise them, we attempt to control them, we suck all the life out of them and make them bland. She talks about native American languages using verbs rather than nouns when describing beings - so "look at that tree" becomes "look at her being a tree". Suddenly the generic fixed tree becomes this particular tree in this particular environment in this particular moment - a living, breathing, becoming tree. Things are animated - they come alive.

Free writing (3 minutes)

- "I am a parent" suggests all kinds of pre-conceived stereotypes or boxes that you can try to aspire to or fit yourself into. "I am parenting" - suddenly gives you full permission to be the kind of parent that you already are in this moment without setting up a narrative for how you should aspire to be a parent for the next 40 years. Think of a role that is important to you and write about it in terms of a verb.

Write

- Start a list of all the nouns/labels that describe you in the different areas and times of your life. What do these nouns mean to you? For example, do you beat yourself up because you don't live up to your labels, but find yourself, instead, constantly aspiring to them and comparing yourself with others?
- What you are 'being' in any moment is always a profound expression of life. Write a paragraph or poem describing who/what you are being at this moment in time. Write as if this is the only moment that matters in the whole of your life.

Make

- Collate photographs of yourself from different time periods, with different people, in different places, doing different activities. Is there one label that covers who you are in all of these images (other than your name)? What 'being' can be found among these images?

Do

- Spend some time today living up to your label (friend, carer, employee, customer, daughter, father ....). Then spend some time just being a human, doing what is in front of you to be done. Notice the difference.

17. Reading the tea leaves

Do you remember when fortune tellers used to interpret the patterns made by the leaves dredged from the bottom of your tea cup? It was seen as a way for fate or the universe to communicate with us humans using random images and archetypes. The same notion could apply to seeing patterns in wood grain, clouds, rock formations, even the beautiful patterns found inside vegetables!

Free writing (3 minutes)

- Look at any textured surface available to you right now. Can you see shapes, symbols, objects, beings? Write about them.

Write

- Write freely across the page. Follow your pen as it moves in swirls and curls, up, down and around the paper. When you feel you have written enough, look at the shapes you have made and see what beings or stories emerge.

Make

Here are two different painting techniques to use to generate some 'random' images. You may like to hold a question in mind as you apply the ink or paint.

- Firstly, Hirameki - dropping coloured ink onto wet watercolour paper and looking to see what appears out of the splotches - then defining any images you see with a pen.
- The second technique is inspired by Suzette Clough's Visual Medicine. She uses an acrylic pour using several different colours. Pour the colours onto the paper and gently moved it around. As the paint slowly dries it continues to move and the colours to interact and eventually it evolves into a magical landscape in which all kinds of images are just waiting for your attention and response.

Do

- Choose one of the images from these activities and keep it in mind today. See if it holds significance.

18. Who lives in a house like this?

This activity comes from Anne-Marie Joban's New Creative Journal. She suggests that we wander around our homes as if we were detectives - using a (metaphorical) magnifying glass to examine our environment and making notes on the various clues we find about the person who lives here. It's a fun exercise and can throw up some interesting insights.

Free Writing (3 minutes)

- What impression does your home create? Does it reflect your personality? Do you feel at home in it?

Write

- Write a script for an audio tour of your home. Include information about the locality, the building, the furnishings, any artwork or personal belongings on display. What's in your wardrobe or even in your diary! What can these details tell you about the person who lives here?

Make

- Take a series of photos or make a video tour of your home. Notice what you decide to include and what you decide to leave out (almost more important than what you choose to acknowledge).

Do

- Make three small changes to your home to make it better reflect the person you are. These could be anything from buying some fresh cut flowers to re-organising your kitchen cupboards.

19. Look mom, I'm zoomorphic!

The Lion Man of Hohlenstein is a prehistoric statue made from mammoth ivory between 35,000 and 40,000 years ago. It is the oldest known zoomorphic sculpture in the world, depicting a man with a lion's head. In that time, before humans had separated themselves from nature and placed themselves in a position of dominion over other beings, we often mythologised creatures that were part human and part animal. Think of the Egyptian gods Anubis (jackal), Thoth (Ibis), Horus (Falcon) or the Greek Medusa (snakes), Minotaur (bull) or Centaur (horse). There is the Gaelic Cernunnos, the horned god (stag), the selkie (seal), the mermaid with her fish tail - and so many, many more.

Free writing (3 minutes)

- If you were zoomorphic, what animal (or other being) would you share your body with? It's important that you don't think too hard about this but just see who is waiting to appear. When you have identified your other half, try asking it what it is bringing into your life.

When I first did this exercise a parrot kept appearing in my mind but I dismissed it without any consideration at all because I was waiting for my 'real' animal (which would of course be something beautiful or exciting or powerful). It took me a while to realise that the parrot was waiting patiently for me to notice and acknowledge it. Yes, parrot was my spirit of the day. When I asked what Parrot brought to my life, the answer was "Colour. Wear your true colours in life. Don't hide among the greys and browns. Shine! Also, use your voice. Don't be shy or over modest. Let it all out." What a great and needed message that was – and one that I almost missed.

Write

- Write a myth for your human and your animal selves.
- What wisdom or power does your animal part want to share with you? Write this as dialogue or as a proclamation.

Make

- Draw an image of your zoomorphic self. This could be realistic, collaged, a cartoon drawing or perhaps in the style of a cave painting.

Do

- Spend some time today feeling close to your animal self. Consult with it. See what it wants and what it has to offer.

20. Spelling Words and Making Spells

An acrostic uses the letters of your name, the name of the place you live, the name of something you love (any word actually) and for each letter, you must come up with another word or phrase. You can use this technique like a mysterious spell to bring words and images into consciousness and to wrap them around yourself to keep you strong and safe, well and sane!

Write

- Write an acrostic using your own name. Think of words or short phrases that have some meaning for you.

H umility

A wareness

Z oomorphic

E ndless love

L ightness of being

- Now, using your name or another word that holds meaning for you, try writing an acrostic poem.

H ello in there!

A rise through the air

Z oom high and free

E agle you may be

L onging for the sky and sea

Make

- What images arise from the acrostic spells? Capture them in colour, form, movement, texture, shape. Paint carefully or playfully with abandon. Paint from your inner feelings if possible and not from your intellect.

Do

- Acrostics can take us out of our habitual way of thinking and create space for new thoughts to come in. If you have a decision to make today – try creating an acrostic from your options to see if this opens up new possibilities.

21. Film Festival

When I lived in North Yorkshire, the hotel in my village used to run an International Film Festival one weekend each year. It was a bit Scandi meets Fawlty Towers and held a certain charm. This invitation is about creating your own Film Festival.

Free Writing (3 minutes)

- What kind of festivals do you enjoy? What do you love about festivals? What would you like to change in order to improve your festival experience?

Write

- Write a short piece about your most interesting festival experience (real or imagined).

Make

- Design a poster for the festival of your dreams.

Do

- Start by coming up with a theme – World Cinema or Science Fiction or Horror or children's films or Noir or comedy or period drama - the list is endless (or, as I originally found myself typing "the end is listless!!!"). What kind of festival food and drink will you need to prepare in advance? Are you going to dress up? Do you need to adjust the lighting/ambience at your festival site (your living room)?
- Check out your streaming services (iPlayer, Netflix, Sky .....) and put together a schedule for a day or a whole weekend. You might want to intersperse longer films with some shorter items from YouTube or perhaps a TED talk. Sit back and enjoy!
- If you want to expand this activity – you could invite friends to join you, either in the flesh or virtually. You could all follow the same schedule and meet on zoom for discussions, food and drink in between showings.

This activity could also be used to create a Literary festival, a Music festival or any kind of festival that would interest and delight you.

22. Daily walk

Is there a regular walk that you do most days? To the shops or to work, to school or just for leisure?

Free writing (3 minutes)

- Recollect the thoughts and emotions you have as you walk through familiar territory. Do you have little notions or narratives about certain features of your walk?

  That garden is so perfect, I bet the owner is a real control freak.

  When all the people are in bed, I reckon these woods are full of night creatures, perhaps even fairies.

  What if, one day, a shipwrecked prince was washed up on this beach, still alive?

  Is that a piece of litter, or is it a five pound note?

  I'm sure that door was green yesterday.

  I've never seen a single customer in that shop.

Try allowing your thoughts to expand. Fill your walk with little imaginary worlds and stories.

Write

- Write some short stories inspired by your walking fantasies. Let the stories introduce themselves to you and inform you whether they are fanciful or serious and who their audience is. Gently tend to their birthing rather than bullying them into existence.

Make

- Create a collage that reflects the ambience of your daily walk. It might include landscape details (buildings/fields/trees/roads) or it might include colours and textures that reflect the environment. Be creative in producing something that, however tenuously, reflects the experience of your walk.

Do

- Walk in a place you haven't been to before. Walk with a sense of curiosity about the history and current narratives of this new terrain.

23. You're a hero!

During lockdown I was thinking (as were so many of us) about every day heroes - doctors, nurses, care workers, bus drivers, food producers, bin men, delivery drivers, posties, shop workers and many more, who all worked with courage and kindness. This led me to think about other kinds of heroes: mythological, historical, literary, comic book ....

Free writing (3 minutes)

- Think about movie and comic book super heroes that you have come across. Which mythological super heroes have you been drawn to? What about historical super heroes?
- What kind of super hero would you be? What would your super power be? What would be your gift to the world?

Write

- Write a Day in the Life of ..... (the super hero you would be). Imagine that your hero lives in your current home and has your current set of friends and family. Write in the first person.

Make

- Create an image of the super hero you are drawn to.
- Make a model (a mini statue or monument) of your super hero using found objects.

Do

- Visit a museum, art gallery or library and get some inspiration around heroes.

24. The Sky's the Limit

If money, time, talent, energy, opportunity were no object - what would you bring into your life?

Free writing

- Think about what would make you happy. What would you choose to own? What would you choose to do? What would you want to be a part of? Where would you spend time? Who with?

Write

- Produce an itinerary or schedule for your perfect week. The sky's the limit. Every item on this schedule is designed to bring you happiness.

Make

- Cut out words and images from magazines to create a collage - lose yourself in the things you love for an hour or so.

Do

- Are there any elements of this perfect life that you could bring into your real life today or this week or this year?
  – I would love to open an animal sanctuary but don't have the funds – I can however, volunteer time at the local cat rescue centre.
  – I would love to dine at a 5 star restaurant but don't have the funds – I can however, splash out on a couple of luxury ingredients for my meal this evening.

25. Critics, Saboteurs and Wise Ones

Julia Cameron (The Artists Way) has written about her inner critic, Nigel, who is an interior decorator with a posh British accent, and nothing Julia does will ever be good enough for Nigel. She also talks about Rolph, who is like a character from Game of Thrones and he knows exactly how to deal with Nigel.

Free writing

- Have a little search around inside your head to see if you can find your inner critic or saboteur and also a more helpful character or Wise One who would support you in dealing with them. Give each a name, a profession, a nationality .... and a few personality traits.

Write

- Invent a dialogue between your critic/saboteur and your wise one. Let them each listen deeply to what the other has to say. Let them each respond honestly.

Make

- Create a cartoon representation of your critic/saboteur. Enjoy having total control over them! Then draw your Wise One – draw them larger and more colourful than your critic/saboteur.

Do

- Take your critic for a little walk. Let him/her know that you appreciate their opinion but mention that they really don't need to shout so loudly in order to get your attention.

26. "Call me by my true name"

Zen Buddhist teacher Thich Nhat Hanh wrote a poem with this title. In it he suggests that many of the names by which life arrives in this world are latent in all of us: the mayfly and the bird that swoops to swallow the mayfly; the frog and the snake that feeds on the frog; the skinny Ugandan child and the arms merchant selling arms to Uganda; the refugee girl and the pirate who rapes her; the man of political power and the man in a forced labour camp ... the last verse is:

Please call me by my true names
So I can hear all my cries and laughter at once,
So I can see that my joy and pain are one.
Please call me by my true names,
So I can wake up
And the door of my heart
Could be left open,
The door of compassion.

It's a poem that faces up to the ugly truth alongside the beautiful truth. It suggests that we don't pick and choose when it comes to how we show up in this world – but it needs to be with compassion, understanding, acceptance of ourselves and forgiveness for others.

Free writing (3 minutes)

- Think about your own true names, even/especially the names that you're not proud of. Try to enfold those names in understanding, tenderness and compassion.

Speaking our true names releases something, loosens the knots, cuts the ties that prevent us from expanding into our true shape.

Write

- List your own True Names – use your non-dominant hand. Write in big letters. Write in straight lines and wonky lines. Write randomly across the page.

My own names include: Acting with Kindness, Going the Extra Mile, Always Smiling, Peacemaker, Bringer of Humour. But also: Cold Shoulder, Impenetrable Shell, Unrelenting Digger-in of Heels, Withholder of Love in Times of Need.

- Write your true names into a poem

Make

- Find images that reflect your true names and arrange them into a collaged shape that feels like your true shape – a circle, oval, square, diamond, triangle or an organic shape that defies definition.

Do

- Do one action today that expresses one of your true names.

27. Beloved Garments

I've had a strange relationship with clothes throughout my life. In my wardrobe I have clothes in a style that I love but don't dare to wear, a style that is so comfortable but not allowed at work, a style that is smart enough for work but not really me. I'm easily taken in by adverts for quirky fashion, styled in a way that looks amazing on skinny, young models with great tans.

Free writing (3 minutes)

- How important are clothes to you?

Write

This is an invitation to brainstorm a series of lists:-

- Which items in your wardrobe please you?
- Which items do you imagine please others?
- What impression are you trying to make? What image are you trying to create?
- Are you trying to convince yourself or others that you are a particular type of person? Are your clothes a disguise or a useful indicator of who you are?
- Left to your own devices – what would you wear most of the time? (pyjamas for me!)

Make

- Search through magazines and catalogues for clothes that appeal to you. Cut them out and create a collage – a kind of mood board that expresses your preferred styles, colours, textures, shapes.

Do

- Look through your wardrobe for items that you absolutely love - and wear at least one of them today.
- While doing this activity, you may notice some items of clothing that you really don't like very much. If practical, get rid of them today. Take them to the charity shop, they may become someone else's much loved item.

28. ZOOM - but not as you know it!

When I start to get niggled and feel that all is not well (the sort of feeling that threatens to turn into anxiety) - it is often because I am overwhelmed by what I am thinking about. The world around me is getting too complicated, too hard to deal with - the possibilities for catastrophe circle me and start to close in ...... That is the time to ZOOM in and focus on one tiny aspect of what is before me. I look at something (anything) and try to see it afresh as an alien might see it.

Canadian academic, John Vervaeke uses the term 'de-automatisation' – using a conscious pause to disrupt the habitual framing of our thoughts and allowing us to find a new and better fit.

Free Writing (3 minutes)

- Think of something that can put you into overwhelm. Start writing. Blurt out every thought that comes into your head. These thoughts don't need to make sense. Just get them out.

Write

- Write a Haiku in the rhythm of 5:7:5 syllables
    - Zoom in on an object and try to capture its essence
    - Zoom in on an emotion that you are feeling
    - Zoom in on the last thought that went through your mind

Make

- Draw or paint a tiny fragment of something in your present environment. Perhaps the skin of a piece of fruit or the woodgrain on a piece of furniture or a button on your shirt.
- Take a close up photograph of something you can see from where you are sitting right now. Move the lens slowly across the surface until you find a detail that really catches your attention.

Do

- Take a Mindful Pause. Stop your endless stream of thoughts for a moment and re-focus. Zoom in on one sense (vision, sounds, taste, smell, touch) or turn inwards and zoom into one part of your body. Allow what you have focused on to fill your whole universe for a moment.
- Play a few notes on a piano or listen to a short extract from a piece of music.
- Dance, limiting yourself to one or two repeated movements or steps.
- Sing a favourite line from a song or read a favourite line from a poem.
- Eat something simple, like a raisin. Hold it in your mouth. Really feel the texture and taste the flavour.

29. Give and Take

The natural flow of the world is based on reciprocity. Plants breathe in our carbon dioxide and breathe out oxygen. Flowers provide nectar for bees, who then pollinate other flowers. Birds eat seeds then poop them out at a distance from the original plant so they can grow. Everything has something to give and something it needs to receive. We humans seem to have dropped out of this reciprocal arrangement because we have substituted money and commerce for heart felt actions and natural ways of being. When our value in this world is seen in monetary terms, we become disconnected from our true place in the natural order.

Reciprocity is not about being good – it's about finding joy and feeling fully aligned with a meaningful life.

Free Writing (3 minutes)

- What does reciprocity mean to you?

Write

- Start a gratitude list identifying everything you have received today. Be specific and include the air that you breathe, food, shelter, transport, kindnesses, health, your environment, inspiration.
- List all the ways in which you reciprocate that do not involve money (for example watering your plants, telling the birds how beautiful they are, smiling at a stranger, doing some volunteering, picking up litter, making a picture or a poem or singing a song).

Make

- Find some coloured or patterned card – cut it into pieces (approximately 4 x 8 cm) and write one reciprocal action on each. Use the cards as reminders for action you can take when you're running on empty.

Do

- Do something selfless within the next 5 minutes.

30. Neurons that fire together, wire together

I'm not a neuro-scientist, but even at my simple level of understanding, it's plain to see that our regular, constantly repeated thoughts become the foundations of our reality and form the basis of all our choices and decisions which then give shape to our lives. By creating new, more positive thoughts we begin to de-fuse old and unhelpful habits.

Habitual thoughts might include: I'm not good enough, I don't deserve to have the things I want, I have no skills or talents, I'm unattractive, no-one would like me if they knew what I was really like ...... these seem to be quite common 'wired together' neural pathways for many people.

Free Writing (3 minutes)

- Blurt out any habitual thoughts that come into your head. These may be thoughts about yourself, your friends and family, your employer, the government, corporate companies, your philosophy, how things work or should be done, the meaning of life ....

Write

- One way to begin to re-wire your brain is to list (in big writing) some of your negative beliefs and then to counter each one. A little trick to wrong-foot your tightly wired neural pathways is to write the list with your non-dominant hand.

For example: 'I'm not good enough' might become 'I don't always get it right, but I'm not aiming for perfection'.

Make

- Write one of your new thoughts using hieroglyphics.
- Make an illustrated poster for your new thought.
- Imagine a map of your brain and colour in the new neural pathway.

Do

- Establish the new thought by reinforcing it in whatever way you can, as often as you can, until it becomes a deeply rutted highway in the landscape of your brain. You could write the new thought as lyrics for a song and then allow it to become this week's earwig. You could proclaim it in the form of a poem. Give it a rhythm and dance it. Turn it into a mantra and repeat it on your daily walk.

31. What's in your shed?

Since childhood, I have always loved the idea of living in a tree house or a beach hut or on a canal boat or, best of all, in an ancient garden shed at the bottom of a secret garden. These fantasy places feel safe, secure and are totally bespoke to my own needs and wants – and, being so small, home to sufficiency rather than to greed and consumerism.

This is another idea inspired by Anne Marie Jobin's New Creative Journal.

Free Writing (3 minutes)

- What kind of shelter would you love to make your fantasy home in?

Write

- List all the things in your life at the moment that help to keep you healthy in body, mind and soul. These may be circumstantial things like access to clean water and fresh air, or they may be intentional things you bring into your life - books, nutritious food, yoga, music, art ..... all the things, people and other than human beings, that soothe and nurture you.
- List all the things in your life at the moment that will definitely not be allowed within a hundred miles of your shed.

Make

- Take a large piece of paper and collage an environment that nurtures you.
- Draw or find an image of a shed that appeals to you. Place it in this environment – stick it down so that you can lift it, like a flap, to see what's inside. From a magazine or your own photo album, cut out and collage things from your nurture list and place them safely inside your shed.

Do

- Find a way to recreate aspects of your 'shed'. An area (either inside or outside your current home) where you can create a cosy nest. It might be an armchair or a park bench. Or make a mini shed in a shoe box and place some nurturing items inside.

32. Becoming

"All land left to its own devices wants to become wood" so says Mary Reynolds (The Garden Awakening). Wasteland, wheat fields, pasture land, bogs, air fields, gardens, cemeteries, prairies - all land wants to become woodland - and of course, once upon a time, before humans had the technology to change things, most of the land was covered in trees. This quote made me wonder, what do all humans naturally want to become? Artists, prophets, wilderness seekers, hearth tenders, warriors, powerful leaders, tyrants, saints or sinners? Without the hefty constraints and influences of our culture - what would humans naturally long to be?

Free writing (3 minutes)

- Looking to mythology, archetypes, fantasy tales, the imaginal world for inspiration - what kind of human do you long to become? Left to its own devices, what do you envision the whole of humanity becoming?

Write

- Compose a quote that sums up your thinking about what it is that humans long to become.

Make

- Create an image that clearly expresses what all humans left to their own devices want to become....

Do

- Sit quietly and visualise yourself as a tree – feel your roots firmly planted in the ground, feel the strength of your trunk supporting branches that reach out to the sky.
- Now, visualise yourself as a bird – feel the lightness of your body as you stretch your wings and soar through the air, the gentleness of your arrival as you alight on a branch, feel the opening of your throat as you release your full-throated birdsong.
- Finally, visualise yourself wherever you are at this moment. Feel the weight and density of your body, the complexity of your thoughts, the emotions springing from your heart. Ask yourself again, what is it that I, left to my own devices, want to become?

The process of visualising is very personal and you may wish to adjust this exercise to fit your unique preferences. Some people find it easier to visualise inanimate beings, such as mountains or rivers or stars. If you have difficulty with visualisations, you might try using sounds – if I was the sound of bells ringing or the breeze rustling through leaves or waves crashing on the shore .

33. Good Intentions

Intentions are different from goals. Intentions are ways of being, whereas goals are end products. An intention is like a stream - it meanders between banks, around rocks, under bridges, it ripples against paddling feet, it carries small creatures, it flows into spaces and is easily pushed out of others. A goal on the other hand is often relentlessly pursued. If it comes across an obstacle it deals with it, it problem solves, it is tenacious, one pointed, focused. We need both intentions and goals in our lives, but it's best not to confuse the two.

Free Writing (3 minutes)

- Think about the goals that you have pursued in the past. How has success or failure affected the course of your life? Try to think of one lasting consequence.

Write

- Make a list of intentions for today (*be kind to myself, connect with others, be nourished by nature, be honest in my dealings, live from my heart).*
- Make a To Do list of things (goals) that could support your intentions (*have 10 minutes lazing in bed before getting up, phone my sister, buy a pot plant for the kitchen windowsill*).

Make

- Choose an image to represent your intentions for the day. It might be a place or a person or a situation or an event or an activity or perhaps a symbolic talisman.

Do

- If you have an altar, place something on it that will represent your daily intention.
- As you head into your day, hold your goals lightly and let your intentions lead the way.

34. Who are They?

As our minds gallop through the day like some frantic horse on a mission, we often have a sense of a great *them* out there who know exactly where we are headed (and what time we should be arriving). We hope that we are doing well enough on our journey and try hard to gain *their* approval.

Free Writing (3 minutes)

- Who are *they*? For some people *they* might be deities, for others, ancestors. *They* might be our family or community or society – the people who lay down the guidelines with which we try to comply. *They* might be internalised voices from the past or the voices of teachers or leaders and influencers – the marketing departments of every company in the world!

Write

- What do you wish *they* would say to you? What recognition or acknowledgement would make you really happy? Write a letter to yourself from *them* affirming all the things you long to hear.

Make

- For this collage you need to find an image that can symbolise you – and stick it in the centre of a sheet of paper. Then surround this with images that symbolise *them.*
- If you have chosen images that are comforting and healing, add some nurturing words cut from magazines to express this.
- If the images are less friendly, cover *them* (obliterate *them*) with a coat of gesso or thick paint in a colour that you find soothing. Once the paint has dried, add some nurturing words and images cut from magazines to express comfort and healing.

Do

- As you go out into the world today, remember that you might be *them* for the people you meet. Be gentle and listen out for what they need from you.

35. Crossing the Line

I sometimes see my life as a kind of tight rope or line that I wobble about on trying to keep my balance.

1. Life 'on the line' is very simple and nourishing (good food, meditation, journaling, walking, reading, listening to music, cuddling my cat).
2. I also have a life 'above the line' where my aspirations live (being a published author, being a successful song writer) – these can feel quite demanding and sometimes risky.
3. Then there is life 'below the line' where I indulge in things that are not very nourishing but I just want to do them anyway (eating too much cake; staying in bed all day watching box sets; spending time immersed in my little screen when I could be out in the woods).

All three layers are important components of my life, but it is helpful to know which activities to turn to when I'm feeling confident, which activities to turn to when I'm in need of solace and which activities to turn to when I want simplicity and consolidation.

Free Writing (3 minutes)

- What is the line that you are walking in your life? Perhaps there is more than one line?

Write

- Divide a sheet of paper into three horizontal columns headed: Above the Line; On the Line; Below the Line. Generate lists that fit into each category.

Make

- Draw or paint an image that expresses 'the Line' for you.

Do

- Do one thing to help you to regain your balance on the tightrope of your life today.

All About Me – Selfies

This whole book is an invitation to think about 'me'. Not 'me' in an isolating, egoic sense, but an invitation to clarify thoughts, feelings, views, values and beliefs in order to live your best life. Here is a short section where you might like to have some fun creating journal selfies.

36. Me is in Metaphor

For this exercise, let your mind roam freely and don't think too hard about it. Invite the metaphors to become strange and weird and in doing so, get more and more clues about how you really see yourself.

Free Writing (3 minutes)

- How are you feeling right now? Use single words or short phrases.

Write

- Write a list of 'I am .....' using metaphors and similes.

I am weak as a torn leaf blown by the storm

I am the crest of a wave

I am a small ship guided by bright stars

I am a tapestry - worn and faded in places, vivid and bright in others

I am a flower growing unnoticed by the motorway

I am a chord played quietly

Make

- Use one of the metaphors from your list and create an illustrative image. You could cut pictures from a magazine or produce your own. Write a poem around the edges of your image (like a frame).

Do

- Create metaphors for everyone you meet today (include animals and birds and insects if that pleases you).

37. Endangered Species!

World famous anthropologist talks about humans, the most recent species on the endangered list!

You can make this a wild and wonderful activity - what you write doesn't have to be true. Sometimes you learn more about yourself when you wander off into your imagination.

Free Writing (3 minutes)

- What are the cutest things about you? What sweet little habits do you have? What's funny or curious about your behaviour at times?

Write

- Write a selfie in the documentary style of David Attenborough.

Homo sapiens, or humans as we know them, are highly intelligent primates and have become the dominant species on earth. Here we find one particular human engaged in a ritual called 'doing the laundry'. We can see, from the items hanging on the washing line (colourful long skirts and tie dye T-shirts) that she is a single female and that she was probably once part of the sub-group known as 'hippies'. As we follow her into the kitchen, we notice jars of grains and pulses on the open shelves suggesting that she might be a vegetarian - this is confirmed by the empty Vegan Pizza box in the re-cycling bin .....

Make

- Create a collage reflecting your environment, your eating habits, your lifestyle. You may want to include old photographs or documents, ticket stubs or brochures as well as images from magazines, catalogues and leaflets.

Do

- Watch a programme about an endangered species. If you feel so inclined, do something to support the World Wildlife Fund or a similar organisation.

38. Letter of Introduction

The letter of introduction was an essential component of polite social interaction in the 18th and 19th centuries in Europe and would have been used, mainly, to present your credentials in business circles.

Free Writing (3 minutes)

- Think about the last time you wrote or received a letter. What was the content? What was the purpose?

Write

- Write a letter of introduction for yourself. In the spirit of tradition you might like to include:
  - details of your appearance (including your style of clothing)
  - important aspects of your background and personal history
  - the activities and interests that you are drawn to
  - the things that cause you concern in the world
  - a description of your environment (home, community, society, culture)
  - the work you do (paid or unpaid)
  - something about the important people in your life (you may know these people well or they may be people who have influenced you through their work or views).

This is a substantial piece of work - you may want to write it fairly quickly and then come back to it later, re-read what you've written and add more detail. What I learned from doing this myself was not so much in the detail (I already knew this information), but in noticing the mass of information that I had chosen to exclude.

Make

- Decorate an envelope in which to keep your letter. This might be a traditional envelope or a design that you have created yourself.

Do

- Write today's date, in pencil, on the outside on the envelope and place it somewhere safe. Re-read the letter in one year's time. Make adjustments or additions as appropriate.

39. Waving or drowning?

Throughout history phenomena have arrived in waves – forming, building, mounting, cresting, crashing ... then forming again. Waves of war, famine, disease, death. We might blame humans for creating these waves and we might think that humans can stop the waves - but that notion suggests that we are gods rather than the fairly helpless bipeds we truly are. I think the same is true in our personal histories. Waves naturally rise and fall and sometimes crash tumultuously. Often we try our best to maintain a calm sea, but that is against nature - waves are what make our lives interesting. Waves are where we build our strength and learn how to swim. Waves are where we discover the richness and meaning of our lives. How we ride our waves determines the course of our lives.

Free Writing (3 minutes)

- How is the ocean where you are today? Is your life gently lapping or is it shaking with disruptive waves?

Write

- Write a list of the disruptions (waves) in your personal history.
  New life, death of a loved one, marriage or romance, endings and divorce, moving home, changes at work, unexpected events, health issues, peak experiences, spiritual experiences, life changing lessons, memories that stand out.
- Circle the events that you feel went to the very core of you. How have they shaped you? How have they shaped the course of your life? How have they shaped your beliefs - about yourself? About others? What was the learning?

Make

- Is there an image that captures how you feel about the changes and transformations that have happened in your life? Draw or paint your own ocean.

Do

- Visit the sea or find a video clip on a media channel such as YouTube. Listen to the sound of the ocean. Let your breathing synchronise with the rise and fall of the waves, the ebb and flow of the tide.

40. 100 Years of Big Birthdays

This prompt invites you to reflect on a lifetime of memories and hopes, embarrassments and enlightenments.

Free Writing (3 minutes)

- What is your earliest memory? Try writing with your non dominant hand for a few minutes.

Write

- List the big birthdays – 10, 20, 30, 40 ..... and take yourself back in time trying to remember what was going on for you at that point in your life.
- Project into the future and imagine how the list will continue.

When I was ten, I was so disappointed that I still had to go to bed at eight o'clock after Coronation Street.

When I was twenty, I knew everything there was to know.

When I was thirty, I was confused about whether or not I had achieved my potential or whether I needed to try harder.

When I was forty, I was plucking fruit from higher branches - much higher than I had thought possible.

When I was fifty, my cup overflowed, I gave the cup away and ran off to the mountains.

When I was sixty, I was perplexed when younger people gave up their seat for me on the bus.

When I reach seventy, I will probably be perplexed if they don't.

When I'm eighty, I'll regret not buying that flat with a view of the sea.

When I'm ninety, I'll regret nothing as I sit with my cat on my lap and a cup of tea.

When I'm one hundred years old, I'll walk into the forest and sit with my back against a tree and happily wait for it all to be over.

Make

- Create an image of the birthday cake you would like to receive for your next big birthday. Let the theme or decoration relate to the decade you are currently living.

Do

- If you are really clever, perhaps you could actually make the cake.
- Alternatively, buy yourself a birthday present. Let it be something you would have really appreciated for one of your past big birthdays.

41. Note to Self

Writing letters (never meant to be sent) can be cathartic and eye-opening.

Free Writing (3 minutes)

- What's on your mind? What's bothering you at the moment? What would you like to unload? Spit it out in words, phrases, exclamations!

Write

- Write a letter to a physical part of yourself. This could be to a part of your body or an illness in your body - let it know what you have noticed about it, how you feel about it, what you would like your future relationship to be with it *(I wrote to my breast cancer when I was diagnosed in 2012 - it was a very illuminating and empowering experience).*
- Alternatively, you could write to a quality that you feel is your stumbling block in life - the thing that always holds you back. This might be your shame or your ignorance or your selfishness. This writing can be a way to get more clarity and perhaps to bring a little compassion and understanding to these areas.
- Once you have written your letter, write a reply. Use the first person to respond from your body part, illness or quality.

You might like to use illegible writing for this exercise. This is a technique where you write 2 or 3 lines then write over the top of them – so the writing becomes indecipherable. It's a good technique for writing secrets or for topics where you carry shame.

Make

- Create an image of the recipient (body part, illness, quality). You might anthropomorphise them into human form or they might be a more abstract manifestation.

Do

- Take any wisdom or insights that you have discovered and write them onto sticky notes. Place them around your home – notes to self.

42. Note to Another

Free Writing (3 minutes)

- This is an opportunity to let off steam. Write as many complaints as you can think of in 3 minutes.

Write

- Compose a letter to someone/something you find irritating or frustrating, someone you don't understand, someone who's point of view you find inexplicable .... and then write a reply from them back to you. Try to put yourself in that person's/that thing's shoes - see the world and all of its demands and pressures from another point of view.

I have used this technique in trying to understand politicians, family members and even the ants invading my kitchen!

"Dear Ants, I know I'm back to nature and all that malarky, but I really don't want you in my house and I will take measures if you insist on turning up and crawling all over the biscuit tin."

"Dear Hazel, all property is theft (Pierre-Joseph Proudhon) and in our world the predominant cultural belief is 'survival of the most tenacious'. We have no wish to harm you, but you really can't keep all the biscuits to yourself when you can easily survive without them and there are thousands of us that need feeding. And did you know that we work hard to aerate the soil so that water and oxygen can get to the wheat that makes the flour to make the biscuits? And we also provide food for many other organisms. We're an essential part of the ecosystem (unlike you humans). So please wind yourself back in and let us live side by side - there will always be more biscuits!"

Make

- Now make a beautiful card for your correspondent, thanking them for their reply.

Do

- As in the previous exercise, take any wisdom or insights that you have discovered and write them onto sticky notes. Place them around your home.

Scatter the Seeds, Harvest the Fruit

What turns up when we dig a little deeper? What are your secret longings? Where are the hidden wounds? What provides compost for your vegetable plot, mulch for your seedlings. This section provides an opportunity to identify those things that will support and nourish you as you move through life.

43. Obstacles

Obstacles are all of the things that hold us back from living an authentic life. They could be external situations that are beyond our control, or our own values and beliefs could be getting in our way.

Free writing (3 minutes)

- Focus on where you say 'no' to life - where you say "I don't think I'm capable" or perhaps " I don't have it in me to face this" or "I'm not worthy – I don't deserve this".

Write

- Make a list of the main obstacles in your life.

Make

- Gather together a few pebbles or stones. Using a felt tip pen, write or draw an 'obstacle' on each stone (you can use a symbol if that feels more appropriate).

Do

- Hold each stone in turn, feeling its weight, its temperature, its texture and open to the difficulty posed by each obstacle. Notice how much you feel charged by it - perhaps your whole personality has developed around these frustrations, fears and worries. Take your stones or pebbles to a pond or lake, river or stream or to the sea and throw them one by one - a little ritual of release. Feel a lightening of the load.

44. Blessings

As I write, I notice just what an abundance there is in my life. There is always food on my table. I have a cosy bed to sleep in each night. I have a roof when it rains and a fire in the grate when the north wind blows. I have books to read and music to listen to. I have a few good friends and close family. I have a reasonably healthy body most of the time. I sleep peacefully most nights. Compared with many creatures on this planet, I am blessed with an easy life.

Free writing (3 minutes)

- What are your blessings? What's on your gratitude list?

Write

- Imagine that you woke up this morning homeless, friendless, jobless, no welfare state to be your safety net, bleak weather or perhaps raging heat in the middle of a desert ...... Now write a poem of appreciation about all the things that you would miss from your actual day to day life. Include the mundane as well as the special.

Make

- Write or draw your blessings on pebbles (as with the previous activity)

Do

- Place your pebbles carefully in nature or in a public place where they might be noticed by others, or place them on an altar or in your pocket. Gift them to others or keep them as reminders of your appreciation for the life you have. Surround yourself with blessings.

45. Talisman

I've been walking around for some time with a talisman in my pocket. It's an anchor drawn on a pebble with a felt tip pen. For me, the anchor symbolises something strong and real that holds me in place even when I'm sailing rough seas, being tossed around by my emotions or my crazy thoughts. It also anchors me to the earth when I'm away with the fairies - dreaming or fantasizing. It brings me back 'home'.

Free writing (3 minutes)

- Explore the question, what symbol might hold the magic power of safety and love for you? Bringing your attention out of your head and into your heart - sit without agenda and see what images arrive. You'll know when the right symbol appears - you will feel it throughout your being.

Write

- Compose a short poem or piece of prose from the point of view of your chosen symbol.

I am an anchor, ancient and strong, I hold fast to the truth ....

Make

- Choose a pebble or stone or rock, draw your symbol on it.

Do

- Place the stone somewhere that you'll frequently notice it (by the bathroom mirror, on the kitchen window sill, in your purse or wallet). The symbol itself may be powerful, but also the smoothness and weight of the pebble may be comforting at times of uncertainty, anxiety or stress.

46. Art Collector

It is often said that our hearts connect with the world through art and music. Art is a language through which we can find meaning – beyond words.

Free writing (3 minutes)

- Imagine that money is no object. What kind of art would you like to have in your home?

Write

- Choose at least six items to have in your collection. These could be paintings, sculptures, installations - masterpieces or found objects.
- Describe each one. Why have you chosen it? How does it make you feel? What connection do you have to it? Does it, in some way, reflect your own inner love and beauty?

Make

- Find a way to create your collection. Print out copies of your chosen works from the internet or cut out from catalogues or magazines. Draw or paint your own versions – they can just indicate the original work, you don't need to reproduce an exact copy – you could use the same colour palette or subject matter or represent a tiny detail. Use found materials to collage or to build your own masterpieces.

Do

- Put together a catalogue of your chosen works.

47. Make your bed

William McRaven, former four star commander in the American military, has written a book entitled 'Make Your Bed: Little Things That Can Change Your Life ... And Maybe Your World'. It's a number 1 New York Times bestseller!

Free Writing (3 minutes)

- Think about little things you do that improve the quality of your life each day.

Write

- Write an Ode.

Ode to bedmaking .... Ode to washing up ...... Ode to greeting the postman

Make

- Make your bed as if it were an art work. Take plenty of time over it. Put on freshly laundered sheets. Plump, smooth, tuck and fluff - with awareness. Remember, no-one is looking, no-one will know. You are not trying to impress anyone. You are not doing this out of duty or a sense that you 'should' make your bed. You are not trying to get it right. This is a gift to yourself and tonight, when you go to bed, you will experience such a great sense of self worth, nurture, care and pleasure as you climb between the sheets.

Do

- Watch Admiral William H McRaven on YouTube – Make Your Bed speech.

48. Make it beautiful

During lockdown I was cooped up inside my house for months. I took the opportunity to spend five minutes or so each day beautifying one small area of my home. One drawer sorted, one window cleaned, one square metre of garden weeded, one item of clothing cleaned and repaired, one skirting board washed, one plug hole disinfected, one pair of boots polished, one bunch of wild flowers collected ......

Free Writing (3 minutes)

- Think about the difference (if there is any) between doing house work and nurturing your home.

Write

- List all the reasons that you do house hold tasks and turn it into a poem or Rap.
  (to maintain a particular standard of hygiene, just because I always have, to avoid the disapproval of others, as an expression of love – for myself, my family, my friends, my home, it's a standard part of my routine, everybody else does it, I can't stand dirt .....)

Make

- Go on a photo shoot around your home. Take pictures of the areas that you enjoy nurturing. Take pictures of areas that you neglect. How do you feel about the different areas?
  There are certainly areas of my home where I am a careless housekeeper – where spiders can safely build their webs.

Do

- Find one small area of your home that you would like to nurture and go right ahead. You are doing this task in order to make your environment more nourishing – for YOU. Giving time and attention to your environment is an act of self-care.

49. True North

I'm often drawn to the ocean as a metaphor for life. I imagine that we sail through life, sometimes on rough seas, sometimes on smooth waters, managing as best we can. Occasionally we see an island or another vessel and we spend some time there. We may have landed on our feet and delay our journey for many years in a place of comfort or perhaps we create a self made prison. We may have a vague sense of direction, or we may know exactly where we are going. As we slow down, we begin to see the bare bones of who we are and what makes life worth living. We look at our compass and discover TRUE NORTH.

Society often demands that, even if we are square pegs, we must fit into round holes - squeezing ourselves out of shape in order to fit in with societal norms or trying to please others at our own expense. How can we loosen up our joints and relax back into our true shape?

Free writing (3 minutes)

- What's emerging in your life that feels really important?
- What are the things that you are happy to let go of?
- How is your journey? What kind of waters are you sailing right now? Are you out at sea? Or are you anchored somewhere? Is it a place of your choosing?
- Are you most interested in finding a direction or a destination?

Write

- Write a poem describing your True North. Start by noticing the sensations in your body, the way you are feeling when you think about where you are on this voyage. What images or words come to mind? (note them down).

  The Yellow Brick Road
  Is turning to rubble now
  Bright flowers push through.
  I thought True North was
  At the end of the rainbow
  A warm hearth waiting.
  But I find it here
  In this trickling drop of rain
  In this dragonfly

Make

- Draw a picture, make a collage or take a photo that reflects qualities of your unique TRUE NORTH. Step into your little boat and set the compass!

Do

- Visit a museum or art gallery and ponder the lives of the historical figures you find there. Are they remembered for finding their True North?

50. Impossible to live with you (but I know I could never live without you)

Being alone for too long drives me crazy. Being with other people for too long drives me crazy. Sometimes we have a choice. Sometimes we don't.

The poet, David Whyte, talks about the conflict between feeling 'besieged' by the demands and expectations of other people and the heart's longing for connection when we are alone.

Free writing (3 minutes)

- Who could you bear to be quarantined with? What is it about this person that you admire? Who has a fine intellect? Fine skills? Fine talents? Fine qualities? A fine heart?
  It could be someone you know, someone famous, a fictional character, an historical figure - or perhaps even an other-than-human being.
- What would you talk about?
- What activities might you engage in?
- What might you learn from this person?

You might find that the qualities you so admire in them are actually the qualities that you are longing to express in your own life.

Write

- Write a piece of dialogue or a description of how it might be to live alongside this person. Imagine a scenario when you first spend time together, then fast forward several months or years. How might the relationship have changed or deepened?

Make

- Find or create an image that represents being 'beseiged' by the demands and expectations of others. When you are satisfied – turn the image into a depiction of the heart's longing for connection with others. You might achieve this by adding words, colour, texture or cut out images. You might cover or blot out parts of the original. Notice how you feel when creating or when changing these images.

Do

- Make contact with someone you haven't connected with for some time.

51. Monday morning blues

For me, the blues are a kind of guilty pleasure. I know I'm not supposed to enjoy feeling blue, but there is something wonderfully self indulgent about it - I can put on some sad music and relish the emotion lapping at me like the sea against a shore. The blues are nothing like the 50 shades of grey depression, or the suffocating green bog of regret, or the blood red pinpricks of anger or the black barbs of anxiety. There is something of sweet heartache and melancholy about the blues - they come from love lost, not from fear realised or anticipated. The blues stand testament to our ability to love and to truly feel our inevitable losses. Monday morning blues may be an indication of the love we have had for ourselves over the weekend and our grief as we shape-shift into the roles we have to play when we go back to work.

Free writing (3 minutes)

- Reflect on times when you have had the blues and try to identify what it was you loved so much that the loss of it made you feel blue - the focus here is on your endless capacity to love.

Write

- Try writing the lyrics for a blues number based on your reflections.

Make

- Make a playlist of all the music that you love to listen to when you're feeling blue. Illustrate it with images that reflect your feelings of love and loss.

Do

- What are some of the self indulgent things you can do to aid your grieving process? Things that provide solace. How can you honour that love, give it time and place it centre stage as you mourn your loss?

52. What would Eeyore say?

There's a voice in my head that likes to have a whine now and then. "*I feel I'm wasting my days. I need to get on top of things again. I've lost direction. I should be doing more. I should be doing less. Who am I anyway?* "

There's a wonderful book by Benjamin Hoff called The Tao of Pooh, which borrows Winnie the Pooh's take on life to bring wisdom into our human world. Pooh's wisdom is awesome, but I've taken to inviting his friend Eeyore to be my inner mentor – his philosophy seems to be much more in keeping with my own outlook.

My favourite Eeyore quote for lockdown: '*I might have known. After all, one can't complain. I have my friends. Was it last week or the week before that, Rabbit bumped into me and said "Bother!" The social round. Always something going on.*'

Free writing (3 minutes)

- Think of a wise old character from your childhood library - choose the one who completely understands your inner child, values your inner child and shares your inner child's world view. What does s/he have to say to you?

Write

- Ask your wise teacher to write a little book of wisdom for you. Provide him/her with a notebook and pen and encourage them to write down all the good advice they have for you.

Make

- If you can find an old copy of the book your character comes from – personalise the book. Blot out words. Add new words. Highlight phrases or sentences. Add photos of yourself, your home, your family, your pets. Give the book a new and meaningful title.

Do

- Write the most impactful quotes on sticky notes and put them somewhere you'll notice them regularly.

53. Courage to Be

This was the name of the first clown training course that I attended. Not Courage to go out and save the world - just the courage to be - without a mask, without armour, without judgement, without agenda, without cleverness - the courage to fully be with my vulnerable, feeling self.

Courage is what it takes to apologise when you've had a row with a friend, or to turn up to work after you've made a mistake or let people down, or to say 'No' when under pressure, or to stay dedicated to a project when no-one seems to care. Courage is about doing what you know is right, against all the odds.

Free writing (3 minutes)

- Where in your life do you need some courage? What do your dragons look like? Where do you feel afraid? What are you avoiding? What step are you unwilling to take?

Write

- Write a micro story (just a few sentences) or a poem, a nursery rhyme, a myth, an ode, a saga – what you will. Introduce us to your courageous inner clown as s/he encounters your scary inner dragon. What do they have to say to each other? What happens next? Write it with courage.

Make

- Find or create an image to represent your courageous clown – remember that being courageous is not the same as being heroic. It is often quiet and resolute.
- Now, find or create an image to represent your scary dragon. This may be an inner or outer dragon. It may be a personal quality or an event or a memory or something/someone very real in your life at the moment.
- Bring them together in a visual scenario that cares for and respects each character.

Do

- Try taking your clown with you into your days and together you might tame some dragons!

54. A Day in the Life......

You are exactly who you are supposed to be. You are not somebody else and you were never meant to be other than who you are - right now. All of those parallel lives belonging to who you could have been if you had made different choices, are all jogging along nicely in your sub conscious, but the life you have chosen to live out here in this world is unique and real.

Imagine a forest, filled with all kinds of trees, where each tree knows and loves what it is with total contentment and would never dream of comparing itself to other trees. How terrible it would be to enter a woodland where the Oak was trying to be a creeping Ivy or vice versa. But that is often how we humans try to live our lives - by comparing ourselves with others and thinking we are not enough.

Free writing (3 minutes)

- Imagine someone is making a movie called A Day in the Life of (insert your name). The protagonist is you – it is important that you are able to be in touch with your feelings, motivations, honest reactions in order to portray this character well (we're going for an Oscar here!) How might you sum up this character?

Write

- Write a synopsis of the film. What happens during this day? What is the main action? What little details bring richness to this docudrama? Who are the other characters? Where is the film located? Is there a shape to the day, or do the hours and minutes trickle by randomly?

Make

- Produce a publicity shot of yourself. This could be a photo or a sketch. Think about the details that will help you to show up rather than hide away.

Do

- Observe yourself today as if you were the star in this blockbuster movie - see yourself for the completely unique being that you are. You don't need to do anything special – being ordinary is beautiful. Be your full-blown self, whatever that is.

55. 'I am the Walrus'

So sang the Beatles in a song that seems to be about the one-ness of all beings - *I am he as you are he and you are me and we are all together.* Looking at events from different view points and perspectives is a great technique for deepening your understanding and strengthening your tolerance.

Free Writing (3 minutes)

- Imagine for a moment that you are a walrus. Write about what's going on in your world today. You don't need a degree in zoology – just use your imagination.

Write

- Look around the space you are in at the moment. Pick at least 5 items and write a sentence (or more) from each perspective.
- Think of a recent news story about a particular person. Write the story from that person's point of view (they may be a victim or a perpetrator, a hero or a witness).

Make

- Produce a picture that tells or suggests a story (draw, paint, collage or photo).
- Add speech bubbles for some of the objects/beings that you have created.

Do

- Visit a museum, art gallery, library, zoo or even a supermarket. Imagine how the world might seem through the eyes of the people or objects that you come across.

56. Headline News

Blow Me Away!

Scientists have developed an elixir that will enable humans to grow feathers. This major breakthrough means that we will no longer need to use fossil fuels to heat our homes, schools, factories, hospitals, care homes and offices – and not only will our feathers keep us warm, but, because we will all be able to fly, there will be no need to use natural resources to fuel transport.

Free Writing (3 minutes)

- Is there a headline that sticks in your mind? Is there a recent news story that caught your interest? What was it about? Why did it impact you?

Write

- Come up with a headline and short article that you would love to see plastered all over the news. It could be personal, local, national, international or even inter-galactic! It can be as realistic or as bonkers as you wish - as long as it makes you happy.

Make

- Using an old newspaper, cut out sections from a variety of articles and collage them onto a sheet of paper to make a new story. You can cut out individual words or a whole column. Add photos or illustrations from the same newspaper. Your new article doesn't have to make sense in a conventional way – in fact, it will be far more interesting if it doesn't.

Do

- If possible, go on a photo shoot to illustrate the headline that you came up with.

57. Into The Woods

In myths and fairy tales the woods are often full of monsters, demons and trolls just waiting to get us. But they sometimes also contain helpers - wise old women who live in caves or cottages, fairies and elves, talking animals or spirits. The woods are a place where we can run away from our fears or face them. If we refuse to go into the woods, then our fears will always be there taunting us.

Free writing (3 minutes)

- Take a look at the bogey men who haunt your inner woodland. See if there are also some benevolent helpers who can offer enchantments or words of wisdom to help you to overcome your fears.

Write

- Write a fairy story or poem Shine a light on the fear inducing creatures that are holding you back from living a full and beautiful life.

There have been giants living in my woods. They are the big organisations I have engaged with, mainly through my work, who have threatened to crush all creativity and humanity out of my soul. They are the faceless corporations who threaten to destroy my home - this beautiful planet – through greed and carelessness. There are also little black imps who cling to my skin - my neuroses - who constantly whisper their negative rhetoric in my ear and distort my world. Then there are the helpers - the musicians, the artists, the dreamers, the poet truth bearers. Those who bring me back to my strength, who wake me up to my truth.

Make

- Find or create an image that represents your wise helper. Place it somewhere you can see it easily (on your altar or by your bed perhaps). Or make a model from clay or dough or felt or knitting and keep it in your pocket.

Do

- Visit some woodland if possible. Walk among the trees in the knowledge that they are living beings. Feel your own benevolence responding to the benevolence of the trees.

58. The Creative Spirit

When I produce something creatively, I feel that it is coming through me, emerging from some unknown territory, carried by some unknown energy that graces me with its presence. It pops out onto the page or the canvas, through my body in a dance, through my voice as speech or song, into the garden or out of the oven. I believe that something universal travels through each of our unique topographies and manifests into this world in very precise ways.

Free writing (3 minutes)

- Sit quietly in front of a blank page, waiting for your Creative Spirit to appear. How do you sense it?

Write

- Describe your creative spirit. What does is sound, taste, smell like? What form does it take? Is it static or changing? Dialogue with it – ask what it needs from you and how you can best work together.
- Once you have a sense of who or what your Creative Spirit might be – write a list of little steps you can take to make his/her/its life more comfortable. What can you do to ease the flow of creativity into your life? How can you be the vehicle that transports creativity into your world?

My list includes: walk every day in the woods, slow down, buy some beautiful pens, write a daily Haiku, read a story to my granddaughter every week – even if it's on face time, try a food item that I've never had before, paint a mandala.

Make

- Try drawing your creative spirit or collaging it. What colours, shapes, textures arrive?

Do

- Play some favourite music. Stand loosely and let your body begin to sway and then to move freely. Let your hands and arms float where they will. Let your feet and legs move as they please. Twist and fold and stretch as the muse takes you. Allow the creative spirit to dance you.

59. Longing and Belonging

What is this longing business all about? The dictionary tells me that longing is a yearning desire for something or someone that is unattainable or distant. Longing is inextricably linked with a need to belong – to find a sense of belonging to our selves, our lives and our world. Longing to be seen, understood and accepted in order to feel that we belong.

Free writing (3 minutes)

- What is it that you long for in your life?
- Beyond your daily needs, what is your soul's longing?
- In what ways do you long to be seen, understood and accepted?

Write

'Longing' is the trigger that starts the journey to 'belonging' - when we long for something, we have taken up one end of the thread, and we can follow that thread to a place where we feel we belong.

- Write a story describing a journey from longing to belonging. This could be autobiographical or fictional.

Make

- Find a way to express your Longing and Belonging as an image - a drawing, photo, collage, installation, doodle, cartoon.

You may already be familiar with an image in a book or have a picture on your wall that depicts your longing in some way. I find the magic, mystery and peaceful presence in many of Jackie Morris's illustrations speak to my longing for belonging in a deep and profound way. Similarly, the highly detailed and atmospheric fantasies of Tracy Savage touch my soul with an intimacy that I crave.

Do

- Spend time in a place or with a person where you feel a sense of belonging.

60. Re-wilding your life

Many of us want to re-wild the planet. We want to stop getting in the way of natural processes shaping the earth and to repair the damage and degradation caused by humans. We want to give nature space to thrive. So how could we apply these same good intentions to our own lives? What would it mean to be able to heal the wounds inflicted upon us by living in a society shaped by huge corporations, where decisions are predicated on what's best for the global economy and the increasing wealth of those in power?

Re-wilding your life doesn't mean that you have to go live on a Welsh mountainside and live off wild garlic (although if that's your thing ....). It may be something much gentler and more achievable from where you are now.

Free writing (3 minutes)

- Recall times when you have felt most in tune with your natural way of being. Times when you have been able to relax, when you have felt connected to life and the planet, when you have felt that you were 'good enough' just the way you are. What (places, activities, people) encouraged these feelings? Perhaps more importantly, what was absent? What (places, activities, people) constrains your natural way of being?

Write

- Imagine your inner garden. What kind of garden are you? Wild and unmanaged? A walled garden - safe and secure? A huge garden that merges with the fields and woods? A balcony garden where magical healing herbs grow in pots? A garden filled with amazing fragrances? A vegetable plot? A minimalist Japanese garden?

Make

- Find a way to capture your garden as an image. Look through lifestyle magazines and gardening catalogues or books. Paint or collage your garden or produce a detailed plan of your garden

Do

- Take a photo of your imagined garden on your phone so that you can have it with you when you walk into the wastelands.

61. Do Nothing to Save the Planet!

Rabbi Jonathan Schorsch has started a global movement to promote the Green Sabbath (www.greensabbathproject.net). A day on which humans can rest, but more importantly, a day on which we humans can give the planet a rest from our constant demands. The Green Sabbath is like the annual Earth Day but on a weekly basis. The focus is on non-action – literally doing nothing to save the planet. Pledges might include: not eating meat, not using transport, not using fossil fuels to heat our homes or to cook our food, not being a consumer (shopping), not using digital devices. Just giving ourselves and the planet a rest on a regular basis.

Free Writing (3 minutes)

- Produce a list of things that you could NOT do that would give the planet a restorative break. Highlight the benefits to the planet and the benefits to yourself.

Write

- Write a short description of what a Green Sabbath might look like for you (along the lines of A Day in the Life of ....)

Make

- Create an image of what the word 'rest' means to you. Breathe into the word and feel it in your body. Imagine that feeling spreading throughout the world then start to paint or draw using pastels or similar. You might want to extend this activity by using other materials and forms – collage, tapestry, clay, fabric, knitting, woodwork or needlecraft

Do

- Choose one or two (or more) items from your NOT list and schedule a Green Sabbath into your life this week.

62. Calling (part 1) What do you profoundly love?

Many of us are interested in what our 'calling' might be. We think of it as something relating to our 'destiny' and if we don't get it right, then we have screwed up somewhere along the way. I have a suspicion that most of us are already following our calling - but we are doing so blindly, without much awareness and without much confidence that we have found the 'right' path. We long for the reassurance of the motorway rather than this vague trail that we seem to be following over the fields and through muddy bogs.

One way to recognise the direction of your calling is to think about what or who you most profoundly love? What or who do you deeply care about? What disturbs or distresses you?

Free writing (3 minutes)

- Imagine that you have a million pounds to donate to a project. What kind of project would you give it to? What is it about this project and its contribution to our planet that you approve of? Does it indicate some of the values or sphere of work that you need to pay more attention to in your life? What is it that really matters to you?

Write

- Start a list of organisations and networks that you are interested in, for example, if you are interested in animal welfare, you might list charities, such as, Compassion in World Farming. If you are interested in the Arts, you might list local galleries or theatres. If you are interested in food or lifestyle, then local cafes or shops might be on your list.
- Brainstorm all the possible ways in which you might support these organisations – financially, volunteering, working with or for them, sharing information on social media, activism ...
- Go through your list and pick a handful of actions that you feel moved to investigate further.

Make

- Draw the outline of a large container on a sheet of paper. It could be a basket or cupboard or building of some kind – you choose. Within this container draw or paste images that symbolise the values you are drawn to in life. They might reflect aspects of your current life or history, or they might reflect aspirations. Find or draw images of things that are very much a part of your life (past or present) that you do not feel nourished by. Place these outside the container.

Do

- Consider the passions and interests that you have identified – pick a handful of actions that you could take today to bring these areas into prominence.

63. Calling (part 2) Making Yourself Visible

What are your most profound gifts? Not acknowledging our gifts - out of false modesty or perhaps a fear of failure, is a form of betrayal. We betray ourselves, but also those who might benefit from our gifts if we were able to offer them more freely.

At some level, consciously or not, you have spent your whole life developing and honing skills and offering them as your gift to the world. You may have focused on one aspect or you may have had a scatter gun approach. All that you give, in whatever way you give, is valuable.

Free **writing** (3 minutes)

- What gifts have others shared with you? Think about teachers, authors, artists, musicians, gardeners, carpenters, carers, protectors ......

Write

- What would be your gift to the world if you had the skill, talent, resources?
- What have you already apprenticed yourself to in this life?
- Which Gods have you worshipped and in which temples have you made your offerings? (metaphorically)

Make

- Take a large sheet of paper and divide it into sections (one for each decade of your life). This could be a symmetrical table or a flowing asymmetrical pattern. For each decade, try to answer the following questions:

  - ➢ What are the skills and interests that you developed?
  - ➢ Where did you put your time, attention, energy?
  - ➢ What did you offer to the world?
  - ➢ What were your dreams?

- Write your answers on your chart. Add images or colours or old photos to bring a richness to this bare bones autobiography.

Do

- Make a commitment to using one skill regularly – everyday if possible. This skill should nourish you and also be of use to others.

64. Calling (part 3) Kneel and Kiss the Ground

"Let the beauty we love be what we do. There are hundreds of ways to kneel and kiss the ground." Rumi

I love this quote from Rumi. It speaks to me of the potential of all actions to become sacred. It helps me to see my responsibilities in life as acts of worship rather than as grinding duties. They are transformed from irritations into invitations.

The indigenous wisdom around reciprocity is strongly linked to a sense of responsibility. There needs to be a natural flow. Breathing in all that we have received (ideas, understandings, experiences) and breathing out all that we give back (through our calling). There is no satisfaction or joy to be had in keeping and accumulating - we need to share the sweeties.

Free writing (3 minutes)

- When you kiss someone, there is both a giving and a receiving within that embrace. What or who in your life kindles that feeling of reciprocity?

Write

- Make a list of the ways in which you kneel and kiss the ground. What are the responsibilities you are holding on a day-to-day basis? (Relationships, home, work, finance, community, health, learning, sharing, supporting). Make sure you include the little things, like putting out the rubbish, as well as huge responsibilities, like the care and safety of others.

Make

- Create a mandala – concentric circles of colour. Place an image in the centre that represents you. Cut out and paste further images that reflect the reciprocal or sacred responsibilities in your life. Add any words that you find meaningful.

Do

- Kneel and kiss the ground. You can take this invitation literally, or find your own way to pause and honour your calling.

65. Synchronising

There is a lovely quote by Steven Foster (School of Lost Borders)

"My soul is striving to remember who I am, to make who I am compatible with who I was born to be, to bring who I am into synch with who I will be."

This 'striving to remember' feels like a great invitation to spend some time synchronising.

Free writing (3 minutes)

- Remembering who I am – that's a profound thought. What comes up for you?

Write

- Get in touch with 'who you were born to be'. What kind of changes might you make to your current lifestyle in order to synchronise with this version of yourself? Where you shop, what you buy, networks you could be part of, informative books and podcasts, work that supports who you really are, investigate your energy supplier, look into animal welfare issues, local community involvement .... Keep writing – this should be a really inspiring list.

Make

- Visualise yourself synchronising – who you were born to be: who you are: who you will be.
- What images come to mind? Try to encapsulate them in an art work.

Do

- Check your list and sit with it for a while. Notice which items you are drawn to, which items excite you and then commit to making one change. If it feels good, make another one change. If that feels good - keep going.

As you do this activity - let it reveal itself to you, don't get into thinking about what you should do (if you were a really nice person). Just see where love pulls you to itself as you transform your life into a prayer.

66. WAKEUP!

A slogan is a short, memorable phrase, nowadays used in advertising. But the word came into use originally as a Scottish Highland war cry! There have been some really powerful slogans/war cries around recently - 'Black Lives Matter', 'I Can't Breathe', 'Me Too' and Greta Thunberg's wonderful 'How Dare You?' I think there is Trickster energy in the world today, shouting so loudly for us to 'Wake Up' and start living as we were meant to live – with gratitude, humility and joy. Many of us are starting to wake up (some were already awake) but are still in that half asleep state of doziness, not knowing quite what we should be doing.

Free writing (3 minutes)

- Write about that state of doziness. What are the feelings, sensations, thoughts, flavours, moods of that half asleep state?

Write

- Come up with a personal slogan (a war cry) - something from the heart, not the head - something that shakes you to the core.
- Write a story or myth where your slogan is the main battle cry of the narrative.

While pondering my own slogan/war cry, "Wake up!", an image of dragons popped into my head. I started to think about sleeping dragons in dark caves guarding their gold - for centuries! And how human greed for that gold has got to the point where the dragons are starting to wake up. They are rising and breathing their fire - a warning shot. But, I'm not looking for a hero to slay the dragon - I'm hoping that the whole of the human race will join together and sing a lullaby that will send the dragons back to sleep, undisturbed, as we find new ways to live - no longer tempted to steal the earth's gold.

Make

- If you identify a slogan that feels completely undeniable, find ways to manifest it in your world. Make a banner. Embroider it into the hems of your clothing. Make a pebble inscription in your garden. Let it be the title of your next song or poem. Design a laminated card to keep in your wallet.

Do

- Take your slogan and write it large. Live with it. Keep it in mind. See where it leads you in your daily actions and decision making.

67. Made-to-Measure or Off-the-Peg?

One of the biggest impacts on me during lockdown was the fact that nothing much happened out there in my usual world – no work, no live music, no films, no coffee and cake with friends, no travelling to visit family, no community events, no art exhibitions or poetry readings - so FOMO (fear of missing out) really diminished in my life. The space that was left quickly filled with things that really matter to me – valuing people and the planet, reading, tending my home, being creative, growing/cooking/eating, spending time in the woods and by the sea ----- I learned how to live a hand-made life, a 'made-to-measure' life rather than an 'off the peg' life prescribed by the story of societal consensus.

Free writing (3 minutes)

- What are some of the things that you do just because of social norms? Actions that are pegs attaching you to the washing line of convention.

Write

- Write about a time in your life when your normal routine was disrupted. Perhaps it was during lockdown, or a time spent recuperating from illness, or taking time out to have a baby, or a period of redundancy from work, or going on a holiday or retreat, or a time when you took yourself off into nature. What insights came? What did you learn?

Make

- Find an image that represents a made-to-measure life that fits your unique values. Contrast this with an image that represents an off-the-peg life that meets external expectations. Can these images work alongside one another? How can you create bridges between the two?

Do

- Imagine that you are an artist creating a hand-made life for yourself. Today is a blank canvas. What activities emerge? Can you do any of them?

Days of Awe

The writing of this book has been a process of finding my voice and speaking out. Why did I need to do this? Because I have lived for most of my life with an inner critic who consistently said, "Who would be interested in anything you have to say? Everything interesting has already been said a million times by people more qualified and far cleverer than you." Then a wonderful life coach, called Matt, suggested, "You may not be the light, but you are a keeper of the light" and suddenly it hit me – I just need to keep on engaging with the process. The outcome is not mine to own – not mine to keep hidden, not mine to promote. The ways of the world are already well documented, but the way that I understand, interpret and translate them is totally original and unique to me. Just as the way in which you receive them will be unique to you. I have been on the receiving end of a wealth of information and wisdom throughout my life and now it is time to make sense of these gifts and to offer them back - brushed, combed and re-braided.

Looking at life through a lens of curiosity and gratitude I can only say 'Wow!' This section looks at what you might call 'the ordinary sacred' that is always here, awaiting our attention.

68. Sacred Journaling

The practices in this book feel like sacred work to me. Creativity is a portal into the Sacred (or perhaps a portal out of the Sacred?). There are many definitions of the word 'sacred', but I experience it as a feeling of awe - a brush with truth, love and beauty – being touched by something bigger than what I already know.

Free writing (3 minutes)

- What does the word 'sacred' mean to you? Can you come up with a definition?

Write

- Create a list of things that are sacred in your life (using your own definition).
- What gods do you turn to? (Nature? Creativity? Literature? Music?)
- In what actions and behaviours do you participate in order to honour these gods?

Make

- Turn your work space into an altar. Use art work or photos, make a collage, arrange some stones or flowers, include a plant, display a favourite poem or prayer. Make sure that everything on your altar is beautiful and has some meaning for you.

Do

- Bring a sacred tone to your journaling - light a candle or burn some incense, play some uplifting music, have your talisman nearby and a warming cup of herb tea.

69. Starting Now

I sometimes think of myself as a vast field of consciousness in which there are unlimited numbers of portals through which I experience life. The portals change as I shift my attention – one moment I'm only aware of my worries or plans, another moment I'm remembering an argument I had last week, and the next I'm here in this moment absorbed in writing this sentence.

My definition of creativity is linked to how consciousness flows through these portals – how we create and shape our lives depending on which portals we are attending to. Any moment can be a time for unfettering and releasing and having the energy to break through into something new. Something more authentic.

Free writing (3 minutes)

- What are your thoughts around creativity? Can you come up with a definition?

Write

- What portal are you standing at right now? Be aware of the sensations in your body, observe the thoughts and feelings you are experiencing. Describe what is going on. Who are you in this moment? What's on your mind?

Make

- Take a coloured pen or crayon in each hand. Using both hands simultaneously, doodle on a large sheet of paper. Do this with eyes closed, then open, then closed again. Do this activity while listening to different kinds of music or at different times of day. Do it slowly, then fast, then slowly again. Let go of control – experience some new portals. When you have finished doodling, you might want to add words or further colours and shapes to bring more meaning to your creation.

Do

- Sit in the garden or any outside space and open your heart to see what feelings and energies might arrive. Sit back – literally – let your awareness float to the back of your head, the back of your torso, the back of your legs. As your mind calms, start to notice what is around you. Let your surroundings take on a very real quality of pristine crispness. Notice that you are the guest here. Perhaps feel the honour of being invited into such beauty, such life, such real-ness. The plants, bees, birds are just getting on with being who/what they are - no fussing about how things should be, how things might be. Feel nature sharing its wisdom with you while you just take your place at this feast of life.

70. Lighting Candles

Sometimes I think about the light and warmth in my life and wonder how it got here.

Free writing (3 minutes)

- Become aware of the light and warmth in your world. Where do you feel it? In your body? Your mind? Your heart? In the air around you? In the objects or people around you?

Write

- List all of the people who have lit a candle in your heart. Write a sentence or two describing what each candle represents?
  Truth? Beauty? Tenderness? Love? Spiritual nurture? Creative expansion? A sense of belonging? Wisdom? Fun? Adventure? Refuge? Forgiveness? Challenge?

Make

- Create an altar of light. Take some flat-ish oyster shells or stones and glue or grout them together to form a tower. Place a tealight on the top shell/stone (I use a bit of blu-tac to keep it safely in place).

Do

- Light a candle for each of the people who have lit your inner candles and reflect on the warmth of the gratitude you feel towards them.

71. Constellations

I don't know much about astronomy or astrology, but I've always been intrigued by the outlines to be found in a starry sky. Ancient civilisations used patterns in the celestial sphere as part of their meaning-making mythologies: Cassiopeia, the Big Dipper, Ursa Minor, Draco, Pegasus, Hydra and all twelve zodiac signs.

Free writing (3 minutes)

- Imagine lying on your back, looking up at a starry night sky. What kinds of thoughts and feelings arise?

Write

- What kind of being would you outline in the stars if you had the power to do so? Write a short mythological story about your chosen being.

Make

- Using a silver pen on black paper, have some fun dropping random stars and comets onto the page - no design, just go wherever your pen takes you. Sit with your 'sky' and see if any images appear - these are your constellations. Use a pencil or crayon to join the stars and bring your constellations into being.

Do

- Visit a library and check out some star maps. Download one of the free night sky apps, such as, Skyview.

72. Unstopper the Bottle

They say that at least 80% of the thoughts we have today are exactly the same thoughts we had yesterday, the day before and the day before that. We ruminate on the same old issues from the past and feed anxious thoughts about the future. We become a stagnant pool.

Doing a daily act of creativity - no matter how small or how silly - somehow removes the stopper from the bottle and life begins to flow again.

Free writing (3 minutes)

- One of the simplest acts of creativity that you can do on a daily basis is Free Writing. What is flowing out of your bottle right now?

Write

- Write a daily Haiku – find the essence of what you are bringing to each day. It could be the after taste of a dream or an intention or a gratitude or a blessing or an awareness ...
- Write Your Own Horoscope. This is something you could do every morning just to get those juices flowing – it may also create some space for you to hear your heart's longings.

Example: Today you'll meet a tall, dark, handsome tree. S/he will fill you with delight and a sense of belonging. Risk your heart and you will be rewarded in ways you cannot imagine.

Make

- Let your own metaphor come to mind – unstoppering the bottle, taking the lid off the box, opening all the windows, bursting out of a birthday cake .... and commit it to paper. See what new thoughts, ideas, feelings are being released. Capture them as images or as streams of colour.

Do

- Take three actions today to break your habits. Actions that you have never done before.

73. Reach High and Bend Low

I went off to the local woods in search of my 'tall, dark, handsome tree' (See 'Unstopper the Bottle'). When I found him he did indeed fill me with delight and a sense of belonging. He also had a message for me - "Reach high, bend low". His upper branches were reaching straight up into the sky and his lower branches bent gracefully down to the ground. This really resonated with my frequent inner struggle to get the balance right - I want to reach high, but not as an ego trip (and my fragile little ego is ever hopeful), I want to fully express the life that is in me, but not as an attempt to validate my existence. And when I bend low, I want this to be with sincere gratitude and humility - not from low self worth or from self limiting beliefs. Well, my wise old tree gave me plenty to think about.

Free writing (3 minutes)

- What does it mean to you to reach high? Who are you at your very best? And bending low - who are you when you take your place at the table of life with gratitude and humility?

Write

- Take a favourite tune or melody. Try writing some accompanying lyrics that express the beauty of reaching high and bending low.

Make

- Create an art work that reflects your humble greatness. Something that suggests beauty, truth and balance.

Do

- Play some music and dance. Let you body reach high and bend low. If there are physical constraints on dancing – visualise these movements, imagine the sensations within your body as you reach heavenwards then down into the earth.

74. True Names

We all live in a normative world where we share a coded language – if I say, "Look at that dog", you will know where to look and what we're looking at. This activity invites you to create a more unique, vivid language – one in which you connect with the world in a much more personal way.

Free writing (3 minutes)

- Imagine an alien has just arrived in your body. It is looking at your hands, moving them through the air, wiggling your fingers, touching things – what might it be thinking?

Write

- Slow down, relax and bring your attention into the moment and, from this place, name the things around you according to how you perceive them.
  So, on my walk today, this oak tree becomes Tall Welcome, and these wood anemones become Smiling Stars, that robin becomes Hopping Red and the breeze becomes Warm Caress.
- This is a lovely activity to do in nature, but can also be interesting and fun to do around the house or in the supermarket or at your work place.
- Considering true names can make your relationship with the world more intimate. Use them in a story or poem or song.

Make

- Here are some of the things in my house – see what they suggest to you and draw them.

  - Place where cat dreams
  - Fire breather
  - Ding Dong just coming
  - Sit space
  - Oggling Box
  - Source of all knowledge

Do

- This is a great activity to do with children, who seem to be so much more attentive to the nature of things than most adults.

75. The Sit-Space

The sit-space is a place you can easily visit on a regular basis, where you can be still, present, undisturbed, able to take your unique place in the world around you. It might be a park bench, a favourite spot on the beach, a rock on the moor, a sheltered spot in the garden, a seat by the window, a meditation cushion...... I have several sit-spaces. They are the landmarks by which I navigate my days - the places I gravitate towards when I want to centre myself and bring myself back to awareness, where I can re-connect with life (my own and the life all around me).

Free writing (3 minutes)

- Where was the first place that you sat down today? Describe your experience.

Write

- Imagine that you are introducing a character in your novel or short story. This character is sitting down somewhere. Describe the character. Describe the setting. Describe the ambience. Keep the description simple and factual.

Make

- One of Van Gogh's most famous paintings was of a chair. Create your own master piece on the subject of your sit-space (real or imagined).

Do

- Choose a sit-space and commit to visit it once a day for a week. Make a conscious habit of sitting and re-connecting, of opening up to the wonders of nature, to the overwhelming sense of enchantment that comes from breathing along with the rhythm of life.
- If you find the idea of just sitting and doing nothing difficult – imagine that you are on a train journey - there is nowhere else to go and nothing else to be done – you are already being carried along in the right direction to your perfect destination just by sitting here.

76. Personal Mantra

I was given my first mantra in 1974 when I 'received knowledge' from my guru at the Palace of Peace in London. It was a well known Hindu mantra - So Hum - translating as 'I am she/that' and meaning that I identify with the universal reality or ultimate truth. The meditation practice was to breathe in while silently saying 'So' and to breathe out while silently saying 'Hum'. This was a very calming technique and I had many peak experiences in those days using this mantra.

I use personal mantras when I feel anxious, (Slow and Still) or if I'm feeling alone, (I love and am loved). I also have a mantra that came spontaneously during a shamanic ritual and which is now engraved into two silver bangles - 'May I be all that I am, with humility, gratitude and joy'. Personal mantras can be specific to a moment of need, or they can be lifelong reminders and supports.

Free Writing

- What mantras have you used in the past?
- What mantra might support you today?
- What mantra might support you in life?

Write

- Choose one of these mantras as the title for a short story, essay or poem.

Make

- Create an image that relates to and includes the words of your mantra. This could be a drawing, a painting or a collage. If the mantra feels particularly powerful, you might want to create something more permanent, as I did with my silver bangles.

Do

- Repeat your mantra out loud or silently while you wait for the lights to change, or while you do the washing up, or when you put the bins out, or as you tie your shoelaces, or climb the stairs. Find one task that you regularly carry out each day and accompany that task with your mantra.

77. Switch channels

There's a lot of information out there about neuroplasticity - how we can re-route unhelpful neural pathways in our brains to increase wellbeing. The more frequently we travel down a particular neural pathway, the deeper that pathway grows – and it becomes the default way to go, like a short cut. It gets more and more difficult to wander down other less travelled paths and roads. We might describe this as reacting to situations on autopilot rather than having a considered response.

Free writing (3 minutes)

- When was the last time you changed your mind about something? How did that happen? What was the process?

Write

- Write a piece of dialogue where one participant seems to be stuck with one way of thinking (a narrow-minded point of view) and the job of the other participant is to come up with as many options and alternatives as possible.

For example: Frances wants to go to Scarborough this weekend because it's an easy train journey and she's familiar with the shops and cafes (and it's where they always go for a trip out). Colin is fed up with going to Scarborough and would like to try somewhere new.

Make

- Imagine your brain as a landscape. Are there deeply rutted, well trodden paths? Is the scenery familiar or are there mysterious areas that you have never explored? Create this image in whatever way seems appropriate to you.

Do

- One simple way to experiment with switching channels is to do so, literally. If you usually listen to Radio 4, switch over to Radio 2 for an hour or so. If you're a pop music fan, give Classic FM a try. If music is your daily companion, try listening to a play or a podcast. Try changing other habits – read a new genre, talk to someone who is 'not my kind of person', eat a new vegetable or fruit.

Changing one simple habit in this way can open the door to changing other more entrenched negative habits.

78. Lugworms

I often walk along the beach at low tide and find little squiggly piles of sand everywhere. These are made by lugworms. Lugworms spend their days tunnelling beneath the surface of the beach, taking in sand through their mouths, letting it pass through their bodies and excreting it as worm shaped castings for me to marvel at when I go for my low tide walks. It's a great metaphor for how we all live our lives - taking in experiences, letting them pass through our mind/bodies and leaving them, somehow changed by our own particular 'shape', excreted into the world.

Free writing (3 minutes)

- As experience passes through you how does it appear in the world? What colours or shapes or textures reflect your unique impact?

Write

- What kind of 'castings' are you leaving on the beach of life? What are the consequences of the way you manifest your experiences?
- Capture your inner lugworm in a poem or short piece of prose.

Make

- Draw or paint your imagined 'casting' and the environment in which you leave it.

Do

- If possible, go to a beach at low tide and examine some lugworm castings. Or go on-line and research these interesting little creatures.

79. Holiday time!

During lockdown I found that not going out was a great opportunity to stay in - meeting the world inside my house rather than going out and engaging with the busyness of life. One of my favourite staying home pastimes, was to plug in my tablet and go on a virtual holiday.

The website: www.seat61.com (or YouTube: The Man in Seat 61) has amazing possibilities for holidaying from your armchair. Click on 'Great Train Journeys' and you can be transported in real time across Australia, New Zealand, Indonesia, California, the Rocky Mountains, South Africa, China, Sri Lanka, the Swiss Alps, the beautiful Scottish Highlands and many other places. These journeys are incredibly fertile soil in which to grow your imagination and creativity. You can travel on the Trans Siberian, The Orient Express, The Canadian and many more. (OTHER WEBSITES ARE AVAILABLE!)

Free writing (3 minutes)

- What are your dream destinations? What is it about these places that appeals to you?

Write

- Write a travel blog about a favourite place that you have visited.

Make

- Tear or cut images from holiday brochures or magazines to create a collage of your dream destination.

Do

- Sit and have a little fantasy about where you would like to be on holiday right now and do something related – eat exotic food, make a cocktail, wear your bikini in the bath ....

80. Transceiver

In the olden days a radio station would *transmit* radio wave signals and our little radios at home would *receive* them. These days, most communication devices include both functions in a *transceiver.*

This idea was prompted by a walk in the woods: the wind was rustling the leaves above, the birds were calling to each other, the bluebells were giving off last gasps of scent as they began to fade but I was only vaguely aware of all of that as background to my 'very important' thoughts (which I can't even remember now). At one point I came to my senses (literally) and really felt the breeze on my skin, really heard the birds singing, really held the fragrance of bluebells in my heart - and it was glorious.

Free writing (3 minutes)

- What thoughts are you transmitting right now? Try to capture them as they arise and write them down before they disappear.

Write

- Write the script for a radio transmission to the nation. Let it be on a topic that is close to your heart.

Make

- Place a self portrait in the centre of a sheet of paper. This could be a stick person, a symbol or a photograph. Draw or paint radio waves being transmitted from you out into the world. Add images or words.

Do

- For one day, try being an old-fashioned radio, and be open to receiving life and all of its wondrous messages. Switch off all outgoing transmissions from your inner radio station and listen in. The key to this activity is to turn up the volume on your receivers (your 5 senses). Let your flickering thoughts and emotions stay in the background.

81. Out there!

Walking in my local park, I was looking at trees and wondering if they have names (personal names). Suddenly, Mabel and Horace popped into my head. I looked at the two trees before me with a sort of question mark in my mind. Yes, Mabel and Horace, came the affirmation. I inwardly greeted them and thanked them for introducing themselves. Then, as I continued walking, Hilda, Jane, Clementine, Esmerelda all made themselves known. I felt a mellow kind of joy and a connection. The next day I met Bruce the Spruce, Dennis, Alice and Agnes. There are so many trees in the park and when I walk there now, I can feel them all wanting to say 'hello'. This is not just my imagination (although I understand that these trees do not actually have human names, nor do they speak English) but I receive the 'being' of the tree and my brain offers up a human name. What's important is that I am recognising the trees as something more than just wood, leaves, blossoms, fruits – they are individual expressions of consciousness.

Free writing (3 minutes)

- Anthropomorphising may just be the way that limited human brains see beyond the 'it-ness' of other beings. Are there non-human beings in your life? Do you attribute human qualities to them or not? How do you relate to animals? Plants? Rocks?

Write

- Try writing an anthropomorphic poem or short story – use anything that appeals, from the blackbird sitting on the washing line to the fridge freezer in the corner.
- When you've finished, ask yourself 'where did this character come from?' And 'what do they want to say to me?'

Make

- Take something non-human (an animal, a plant, your bicycle....) and draw it as a cartoon character. Notice where you include human features and where you think it's important to retain original features.

Do

- In your current environment, what is the human quality of relationship that fills the air between you and your surroundings?

I often feel loved by my home. I can feel dismissed by the shopping mall in town. I feel welcomed by the woods and nurtured by the sea.

82. Touchstones

Black quartz was used in the fifteenth century to test the purity of gold and silver. These metals were rubbed or 'touched' against the stone and the streaks of colour left on the quartz determined the quality of the gold or silver.

Our lives are full of touchstones by which we measure the quality of our experiences. One recent touchstone for me has been the writing of this book. I get up every morning, trusting that something is waiting to present itself on the page - and amazingly, every day something turns up and says "write me". Other touchstones might include time in nature - whether that's a morning coffee in the garden or a walk on the beach or a visit to woodland. A touchstone that is quite mysterious - because I don't understand why it is so important to me - is seeing the full moon. It can stop me in my tracks and fill me with wonder. I keep a moon journal in which I record my life progress at every dark and every full moon. I have touchstone places - both in natural and built environments - museums, churches, garden centres, cafes ....

Free writing (3 minutes)

- What are the touchstones in your life? Name them, honour them.
- How do you test the purity or quality of your experiences, your choices?

Write

- Choose one of your touchstones and write about it. If possible, write in the first person, for example, 'I am the full moon...'

Make

- What comes to mind when you say the word, 'touchstone'? Create an image or representation of it.

Do

- Find something that can act as a physical touchstone for yourself.
- If you have touchstone places – visit them.

I have a smooth piece of black obsidian that I like to hold in my hand as a reminder to wake up when I am lost in thought.

83. Nobody or somebody?

We all experience reality through our bodies - through our senses. Then we filter these sensory experiences through the machinery of our minds and fit them into our unique take on life. But how often do we catch that initial real experience before we judge it, grasp it, deny it, twist it into something we prefer, imprint it with our beliefs and cultural patterns and all the other stuff we do to reality?

Free writing (3 minutes)

- When you first wake up in the morning how do you feel? Is it the same every day? If not, what makes the difference?

Write

- Write a description of a scenario in a short story. Write in the first person. Write from the senses.

  I see... I hear... I touch/feel... I taste... I smell...

Make

- Draw a body outline on a large piece of paper and fill it with shapes, words, colours or magazine cut-outs to reflect your body sensations today.
- Alternatively, fill your body outline with people, events, places that have influenced you – that have formed who you are today.

Do

- Close your eyes. You know your body is still there - but how? What physical sensations can you feel? Are there some areas of your body where you feel tingling (usually hands, feet and face), other parts that feel full or heavy, parts that feel light and relaxed, parts that may itch or feel uncomfortable - parts that you just can't feel at all? There is no right or wrong way to experience this - it's just a 'noticing'. Next time you try, it will be different.

84. Your Inner Healer

A healer is an expert guide who can work with the body's natural inclination towards being healthy. Healers work in many, many different ways with the emotional, physical and spiritual aspects of your life. This is an invitation to become acquainted with your inner healer.

Free writing (3 minutes)

- Find a place to sit and relax. Follow your breathing until you feel that your mind, body and heart are moving in rhythm with your breath. Let a word form with each out breath. It might be a different word with each breath or you may find the same word repeating. Place the words randomly and freely on the page.

Write

- Gently pose some questions to yourself - imagine the questions are like pebbles that you are dropping into a pool of water, the answers will come naturally, like the ripples from the pebble. You don't need to create them, hold onto them, judge them or dismiss them - just observe.

  The questions might include: What does my healer look like? (S/he may be human, other than human, a colour or symbol, a sound ....) Does my healer have a name? What qualities does my healer bring into my life today? What are the obstacles or difficulties that my healer can help me with today? What does my healer want to tell me today? What does my healer ask of me today?

- Write a dialogue between yourself and your inner healer. It could include some of the questions and answers above – or you might want to ask different questions or offer other reflections.

Make

- Draw an image of your healer or find a symbol that you can carry in your bag or pocket to remind you of the part of you that is on your side and wants only the best for you.

Do

- Find some time every day to be with your inner healer. Offer yourself care and compassion, tenderness and acceptance.

85. Dedicated to the one I love

Recently, as I walked in the local park, I saw an elderly woman sitting on a bench in the sunshine. She was hunched over, head hanging down on her knees. She looked so sad. I watched for a couple of moments, but she didn't move, so I went over and asked if she was okay. She looked up and said that she was fine, explaining that she hasn't been able to get to the hairdresser during lockdown, so for the first time in decades, she is having to wash her own hair and had come out to the park to let it dry in the sun. She thanked me for my concern and we had a moment of connection and affection before I went on my way. There is a saying, something like "Strangers are just friends we haven't yet met" and it makes me think about all the love that lies dormant in our lives because we don't take the time to notice it.

Free writing (3 minutes)

- Who was the last person you had an interaction with? Write about the connection you did, or did not, feel with them.

Write

- Bring each of the following people into one interactive scenario (a party, a book launch, the supermarket check out, a wedding reception). Write descriptive accounts of what is happening, in the first person, from each of their points of view.
  - a person in your life that you have deep affection and care for (perhaps a friend or family member)
  - a person you feel fairly neutral about (the postman or a dog walker you sometimes say 'hello' to)
  - a person you are not too fond of (someone who irritates you or who has upset you in some way)
  - a person you don't really know at all (you may have seen them on TV or social media)

Make

- Create an image of a room full of people – but depict only their hearts, not their bodies. You don't have to use heart shapes – some people might have flowers or mugs of hot chocolate or seahorses for hearts! Make sure that your own heart is in there somewhere.

Do

- Dedicate today to someone you love. This might be someone you know well or someone you don't know but who is in your life - like the bin man or the dog walker who passes your window every day. Find a way to recognise them and to honour them - write a letter or make a card, create an altar, draw a picture, sing a love song, phone or text them, make up a little story about them, hold them in your thoughts... just somehow shine a light on that person today and let yourself feel some love.

86. In Your Element (Part 1)

I've been feeling more and more in my element as I spend increased amounts of time in my home and in the local woods and by the sea. I've been feeling more and more in my element as I wake up each morning and wait for something to occur to me that I can write about in this book. I've been feeling more and more in my element as I've slowed down and experienced life as an empty space opening up in front of me, moment by moment, inviting me to move forward gracefully into its lushness. I'm in my element washing the dishes, doodling and jotting, feeding the cat, putting my walking boots on, reading a poem, making a curry, sitting on my meditation cushion, leaning against a favourite tree and feeling held, singing along to Radio 2, having a FaceTime conversation with my daughter, curling up in my bed at the end of the day and saying goodnight to the stars.

Free writing (3 minutes)

- When are you in your element? How can you spend more time in your element? What things in your life take you out of your element?

Write

- Make a list of experiences that bring you into your element. Turn the list into a poem.

Make

- Make a collage. Let it express you in your element.
- Draw your happy face when you're in your element.

Do

- Choose one item from your list, one image from your collage and bring that into your life today.

87. In Your Element (part 2)

When we say "I'm in my element", we usually mean that we are doing what we like and what we are good at - we are where we should be and we feel in synch with the universe. However, many cultures have used the elements - air, water, fire, earth, ether - to understand the different balances and forces that make up our state of being.

Fire: inspiration, action, enthusiasm, courage, passion, vitality, spontaneity, will, faith, possibility. Fire helps us to face challenges and take risks to heal our lives, our world and other people.

Earth: practicality, solidity, utility, tangibility, concrete thinking, groundedness, stability, patience, self discipline, routine, tradition. Earth helps us to build a safe foundation.

Water: emotions, sensitivity, intuition, compassion, flexibility, imagination, empathy, subjectivity, insight, creativity. Water is connected to healing and healers.

Air: thinking, relating, communication, concepts, abstract reasoning, socialising, wit and humour, broadminded, logic, curiosity, objectivity, intellectual. Air is connected to the thinkers and problem solvers.

The fifth element is the foundation from which all the others are able to exist, it is Ether - often described as Space or Spirit.

Free writing (3 minutes)

- Feel your way into each of these elements and see where you feel uplifted - where you feel connected - where there is a spark of joy. Reflect on how the elements play out in your life.

Write

- The elements have gathered in your body for a Wellbeing Conference. What wisdom might each element bring to the meeting? Write the minutes.

Make

- Find images to represent each element and create a collage of your elemental self. You can move the pieces around, trying out different shapes and sizes until the proportions feel right.

Do

- Find representations of each element to place on your altar (or desk or windowsill).

88. Speaking of Spokes

Mindfulness teacher Dan Seigel uses the image of a wheel in some of his guided meditations. He talks about the centre of our awareness being the Hub and what we experience in the world as being the Rim. The spokes are what we travel up and down - bringing awareness to the world or bringing the world into our awareness. For much of the time, I'm completely out there on the Rim, venturing back to the Hub only in moments when I'm practicing meditation or when the enchantment of nature bursts upon me, like someone shining a torch in my face.

Free writing (3 minutes)

- How does it feel at the centre of your wheel? Where is the Hub of your being?

Write

- Write a children's story about a little creature travelling from the safety of its home in the centre of its universe, along the spokes of the wheel to the great world out there. What happens and how does it get back home?

Make

- Create your own meditation wheel. What colours, textures, shapes are at the centre, on the rim, on the spokes? Draw or paint your wheel.
- Alternatively, take a photo of a found object – it could be a bicycle wheel, a steering wheel, a dandelion clock or any other 'wheel' that appeals to you.

Do

- Visualising the wheel, start in the central hub that is pure awareness, breathe yourself up and down the spokes, becoming aware of your senses, your body sensations, your mental activity, your connection to others, then coming back to centre.

89. Pause and Focus

When taking a photograph, you pause to really look at your subject, you focus your lens to capture the clear essence of what you are seeing, you slow right down in order to be in relationship with the scene/object/being that has caught your attention. Taking photos can be a lovely way to slow down and to become more mindful of moments in your day.

Free writing

- How do you feel about slowing down? How often do you take a pause in your day?

Write

- Imagine creating a photograph album of the things that interest you or that you love. What would be in there and why?

Make

- Your photographs are being exhibited at a prestigious local gallery. Produce a catalogue for the exhibition using sketches or (if you have the technology) real photographs or photographs cut out from magazines.

Do

- Choose a theme that interests you. Spend some time wandering around your home or outside space looking for items that reflect this theme. The theme might be natural - birds or plants or the moon or the weather. The theme might be abstract – circles, lines, tiny things, invisible or hidden things. It may be a colour theme – all things yellow.
- Take some photographs. One of my favourite concepts is that of kinship - really feel your way into relationship with your chosen subjects before capturing them on your camera - enjoy!

90. Birdsong

Walking in the woods, watching the sun dip behind the trees and hearing the birds singing their goodnights, I wonder, what does my own birdsong sound like? How do I give full-throated expression to my life? Birdsong is not clever or well-behaved, it is not better or worse than the next bird's song. It does not depend on financial security or being popular amongst friends or in conforming to societal norms. Birdsong is the clear sounding of a unique life.

Free writing (3 minutes)

- Sit with the stillness and silence within and notice what arises - what is the flavour, the scent, the colour, the song that is the unique expression of your true self as you move through life moment by moment, second by second.

Write

- Compose a poem or a short piece of prose entitled 'Birdsong'.
- List the songs that you have enjoyed singing along with over the years. Write about the pleasure you have gained from them.

Make

- Create an image to accompany your 'birdsong'.

Do

- In what ways can you sing your song? What would a full-throated rendition of life sound like?

91. Sacred Days

There are many ways in which to celebrate sacred days. Days that represent light and abundance. Days that illuminate what is within us all. Some sacred days are celebrated across whole cultures others may be more personal.

Free writing (3 minutes)

- What sacred days do you mark? What religious or secular occasions have become sacred days of celebration for you?

Write

- Write about a day when you felt close to spirit. What was happening? Who were you with? What did you do? Where were you? How did you feel? What did you learn?
  This doesn't necessarily have to be a day of religious celebration. It could be a football match or a beautiful day on holiday or the last time you were with someone dear to you.

Make

- Honour the sacredness of the day by making your own mandala from found objects. A mandala represents the circle of life and the connectedness of all things. Start by painting a sheet of paper with a colour that represents sacredness (or joy or beauty) to you. Place your items on the paper in a pattern of concentric circles. You may wish to add some words that reflect your feelings.

Do

- Traditional activities to mark sacred days include: the lighting of sacred fires (which can be anything from a bonfire to a candle); joining with others in a circle or spiral to sing, recite poems and stories, dance and drum; gathering healing plants; creating a sun wheel or mandala, making a crown of flowers or a prayer stick. Do an activity that is meaningful to you.

92. Wild Child

Carl Jung defined twelve universal mythic characters – archetypes that reside within the collective unconscious. Between them, he suggests, they represent the range of basic human motivation.

Leave a mark on the world: Rebel/Hero/Magician
Provide structure in the world: Ruler/Artist/Caregiver
Connect with others: Jester/Everyman/Lover
Yearning for paradise: Sage/Innocent/Explorer

Free writing (3 minutes)

- Create your own archetype for how you are feeling right now. Give it a name. Describe its qualities.

Write

- Choose a personal archetype and write a speech about something that is meaningful to you (the environment, freedom of speech, equality, world peace, animal welfare...) from that point of view.

Make

- Design a mandala for a chosen archetype. Let it convey the life, history and narrative of your archetype. Mandalas can be geometric and carefully measured, or they can be free flowing and wild.
  Take a large sheet of paper. Find the centre and draw a series of concentric circles. Using these circles as guides (stay within the lines or gleefully cross them!) draw shapes, write words, splatter colour to express your chosen archetype.
- Alternatively, take a large sheet of paper and draw a free-hand spiral. Again, use shapes, word and colour to make a satisfying mandala.

Do

- Choose an inner archetype and let it express itself freely today.

93. Artist Dates

I read Julia Cameron's iconic book 'The Artist's Way' in the late 1980s. The two main tools for creative recovery that she introduced at that time have remained a mainstay of my own journaling practice ever since. Morning pages (3 sides of A4 free writing as soon as you wake up in the morning) and a weekly Artist Date (a block of time set aside each week to specifically and exclusively nurture your inner artist).

In the early days, my artist dates were quite hard work, consisting of activities that I thought would be edifying for my inner artist rather than fun and nourishing. I sat dutifully through many recitals, plays and exhibitions that I had little interest in. Nowadays I take my artist to the beach, to the woods, to a newly opened cafe, to the garden centre, to a book shop, for a walk through a busy town centre or a quiet half hour sitting on a rock by the sea. My artist likes new experiences as well as familiar ones.

Whereas I used to find it difficult to fit in this weekly activity, I now find that we're dating most days.

Free writing (3 minutes)

- What is your initial reaction to taking your inner artist on a date?

Write

- Dialogue with your inner artist. Ask him/her to describe what kind of dates s/he would enjoy.

Make

- Create an image of your inner artist – not one that you aspire to be, but the inner artist who is very real and already there inside you.

Do

- Put some dates in your diary and make sure you prioritise them on your 'to do' list.

94. Horizons

What is on your horizon? We are all walking on a path that leads to the horizon and we have been on this path for quite a while. Sometimes we wonder whether we have taken the right path. Sometimes we feel a deep commitment to the path we have chosen. An uphill struggle provides a view of a wider horizon. The landscape closes in when we're on an easy downhill stroll. We may get lost. We may face indecision. But always, the horizon beckons.

Free writing (3 minutes)

- How many paths currently lead to your horizon? Is the way clear and direct or is it meandering and hidden in places? What can you see on the horizon?

Write

- Compose a poem explaining what your horizon means to you. What is on your horizon? What is waiting for you there? Will you ever arrive on your horizon or will it forever be out of reach?

Make

- Take a sheet of paper and draw a horizon from one side to the other. Do this with your eyes closed and use your non-dominant hand. Hold the pen loosely and do not rest your hand on the paper. Draw the line very slowly and mindfully.
- Open your eyes and look at the shape of the horizon you have drawn. What thoughts or images come to mind? You may feel called to add colour, words, objects or beings to your picture.

Do

- Check out the changing physical horizons as you move through the day. These horizons are the container for your physical space. How does that feel?

Life As a Pilgrimage

"If a person survives an ordinary span of sixty years or more, there is every chance that his or her life as a shapely story has ended and all that remains to be experienced is epilogue. Life is not over, but the story is." Kurt Vonnegut.

All of our lives are filled with stories and narratives – some actually happened as we perceived them and some didn't. I love the idea of the story being over but life carries on. Without the limitations of our familiar narrative, life opens up to so much new experience and wonder.

Anne Lamott's wonderful book 'Help, Thanks, Wow! – the Three Essential Prayers' echoes my own personal mantra, 'humility, gratitude and joy'. In her book, she manages to coalesce into three little words the awareness that we need to: ask for help, experience gratitude and enjoy a sense of amazement.

I want the rest of my life to be a prayer. I want it to be Anne Lamott's prayer: 'Help, Thanks, Wow!'

And I want to achieve this by living the rest of my life journey as a pilgrimage. What do I mean by that? What is a pilgrimage? Here are some thoughts and invitations to explore.

Pilgrimage is usually defined as a journey of spiritual significance to a shrine or place of importance to a person's beliefs. It can be a long trek across counties or countries or it can be a short walk to the local park. It is our intention that transforms a walk into a pilgrimage.

Pilgrimages are often taken alongside other people as a way to re-affirm a sense of belonging and to nurture harmony, unity and the ability to care. Pilgrims are looking for new and expanded meaning for themselves, others, nature, a higher good - leading to personal transformation or healing

The invitations in this section are open for you to explore as you will. I suggest an extended period of Free Writing for each prompt, offering plenty of time for incubation. Then see what is waiting to be born – more formal writing, image making or an intention to actively do something.

95. Where to go?

Think about where you would like to go on your pilgrimage. Start by reflecting on past journeys that were perhaps unintentional pilgrimages. You may have visited ancient spiritual sites - stone circles, burial grounds, giant chalk figures carved into the countryside or perhaps more personal locations – the local cemetery, the venue of your first music festival, the place where your partner proposed marriage. Where would you go on a pilgrimage? And why?

Places Where I Left My Heart

The swing at the bottom of the garden
Behind the rhubarb patch and shouldered by
Michaelmas daisies almost as tall as me.
The Sun in Splendour pub, Nottinghill,
Where you bought me pint after pint
Of Guinness and I felt loved.
Anna Purna base camp
The light of the full moon
The insistence of bed bugs.
The rock that's only visible at low tide
Where the little crabs crawled
And I was left marvelling.
The bed where you lay, eyes closed and cooling
The sound of your breath still lingering
As you finally disappeared.

96. What to take?

Now you have some idea of where you might be going - what do you take with you? What will bring you comfort? Nourishment? Support when you're finding the journey challenging? What would you want in your back pack when you set out on your pilgrimage? Make a list - or even better, draw your bag.

97. Travelling Companions

Who would you take as companions on your pilgrimage?

There have been three recent series on the BBC in which celebrities undertook pilgrimages "to promote tolerance for all faiths and cultures" - The Road to Santiago, The Road to Rome and The Road to Istanbul. One of the most interesting aspects of these programmes was witnessing the relationships between the celebrities - how they supported one another, how they used humour to gloss over difficulties, how sometimes they needed to take themselves away for a bit of isolation, how they challenged one another and how they discovered one another. This was in great contrast to Chaucer's Canterbury Tales and the wonderful variety of stories that his pilgrims narrated.

Initially, I thought I would like to undertake a solitary pilgrimage - or perhaps with just my cat - but forcing myself to think further about some human companions I came up with: Mary Oliver and David Whyte - because poets can always see to the heart of the matter and come up with a metaphor that makes it more easily understandable, so would be good for looking deeply into the spiritual aspects of our journey. Then came Barak Obama for some really stimulating conversations with a man who cares and is courageous and has integrity as well as being knowledgeable about world issues. For her sense of fun, joy, love and understanding, not to mention her ability to provide amazingly tasty food, I would choose Nadiya Hussein. And perhaps I would also enjoy the company of Chaucer himself – to facilitate some story telling around the fire each evening.

98. Terrains to Cross

What kind of terrain will you cross on your pilgrimage?

In The Pilgrim's Progress, John Bunyan's character, Christian, journeys from the City of Destruction to the Celestial City, carrying his heavy burden of sins. He meets many helpers along the way and faces many trials and adventures as he goes through the wicker-gate and immediately falls into the Slough of Despond. He visits the village of Morality, the House of the Interpreter, the Hill of Difficulty where he finds the straight and narrow path to the top. He goes to the Palace Beautiful, the Valley of Humiliation, the Valley of the Shadow of Death, the town of Vanity (where he visits the Vanity Fair), he crosses the Plain of Ease and endures a storm. He is imprisoned in the Doubting Castle where he battles the Giant of Despair, but eventually he makes it to the Delectable Mountains and finally to the Celestial City. Perhaps you can imagine his adventures and challenges from the names given to these terrains.

Think about the kinds of terrain or places that might challenge or aid you on your pilgrimage as you seek your truth, as well as terrain already covered in your life.

99. Holding an Intention

What's the difference between a pilgrim and a tourist?

Pilgrimage helps to illuminate the journey of life by focusing on what really matters. You leave behind the busyness of your day-to-day life and literally 'walk through' some of the issues that are on your mind. Most pilgrims have a specific intention - it may be to discover meaning or purpose, it may be to address a specific difficulty, it may be to follow a heartfelt longing or to achieve some clarity about their relationship to the world.

Whatever intention you choose, this is what will guide your inner journey as you perform the outer pilgrimage. Find your intention by identifying the areas of your life where you have some difficulty or frustration and by trying to identify what changes might help: more insight? a change of direction? nurturing specific qualities? attracting the resources you need? developing coping strategies? healing old wounds/recent wounds? falling in love with yourself? strengthening connection with the earth and with the other beings you share it with?

The past disappears
A single cherry blossoms
In my open hands

100. Who's got your back?

At times you may feel the need for protection on your pilgrimage – whether it's an internal or external pilgrimage, you will face challenges and need the comfort of knowing that someone/something has your back.

Think about who or what might give you a sense of security and protection as you travel: a spirit guide or companion; a cloak of protection; an animal of protection; a talisman to wear or keep in your pocket. Imagine a moment of danger. Who or what would you like to see coming through the mist to save and protect you?

101. Giving back

Although you may go on a pilgrimage in order to receive something (clarity, sense of purpose, meaning, healing, insight), it is a common practice to leave something as an offering when you arrive at the end of your journey – at a shrine or on an altar, beneath a sacred tree, by a holy well, on top of a mountain .... Offerings might be something picked up along the way – a stone or a piece of wood. It could be a talisman that has been kept safely in your pocket during the journey or a precious item belonging to yourself or a loved one. Some people leave their walking boots or a piece of clothing that got them through the pilgrimage.

On this journey of reciprocity – what would you like to give back?

The Creative Retreat

Sometimes I like to dedicate a whole day or even several days to a creative retreat. I often do a full week's retreat around New Year. Here are some ideas.

Preparation:

Plan a schedule. Include themes and activities.

Turn off all social media for the period of the retreat.

Clean the house, do the laundry, change the bed linen, plan meals and buy food, buy fresh flowers, scented candles, bath salts, essential oils.

Prepare an area where you can work comfortably and make sure that you have plenty of writing and art supplies. Create an altar specifically for the retreat.

Bring something new into your journaling practice – if you usually sit when you journal, then try standing. If you normally work in silence, listen to music. If you often work in a tidy, contained way, try allowing yourself to be messy. If your habit is to work indoors, see if there is any way that part of your practice could be done outdoors.

Here is an example of a retreat schedule taken from my own New Year Retreat.

<table>
<tr><td>7.00 – 8.00
Meditation</td><td colspan="2">Silent meditation or guided meditation (YouTube)</td></tr>
<tr><td>8.00 – 9.00
Journal with daily themes</td><td colspan="2">Monday: Moon – feelings, creativity, essence
Tuesday: Mars – movement, action, energy, desire
Wednesday: Mercury – the arts, communication, curiosity
Thursday: Jupiter – abundance, luck, expansion, growth
Friday: Venus – love, care, nurture, restoration
Saturday: Saturn – discipline, facing responsibility
Sunday: Sun – spiritual love, compassion</td></tr>
<tr><td>9.00 – 10.00
Nesting and nurture</td><td>Breakfast</td><td>House and Garden tasks</td></tr>
<tr><td>10.00 – 12.00
Creative activity</td><td colspan="2">Monday: Photo shoot in house, garden or local area. Give each image a title suggestive of the feeling it evokes or the story it might tell.
Tuesday: Visualise a fantasy creative mentor. Let them tell you a story and then capture it on the page (words, doodles, scribbles)
Wednesday: Write the lyrics to a song (use a melody that you already know and love).
Thursday: Review the past year. Read through old journals. Use collage to record memories and revelations. Draw/collage a self portrait of who you think you were in this past 12 months.
Friday: Write a chain of thought in Haiku form – like a string of pearls. Let the last line of each Haiku prompt the start of the next.
Saturday: Looking forward into the new year, create a vision board or a mandala that contains the seeds and dreams for the next 12 months.
Sunday: Brainstorm a list of at least 52 Artist Dates for the coming year. Write each idea onto a card and place in a creativity box or pot ready for use.</td></tr>
<tr><td>12.00 – 1.00
Walk</td><td colspan="2">A mindful walk – pausing, taking your time, letting your feet ‘kiss the ground’ (Thich Nhat Hahn)</td></tr>
<tr><td>1.00– 2.00
Lunch</td><td colspan="2">Mindful light lunch</td></tr>
</table>

2.00 – 5.00 Artist Date	Monday: Choose someone you admire (artist, scientist, spiritual leader, activist) and research them – go to museum, library, art gallery, online etc. What do you most admire about them? How can you bring that quality into your life? Tuesday: Go for a picnic – take a poetry book. Wednesday: Sort out bookshelves and put together a reading list for the next year. Thursday: Design a self care package and pamper yourself. Friday: Do something niche/speciality. Visit a niche museum. Go to the library and research a niche subject. Eat at a niche cafe or restaurant. Go to a niche shop and buy something. Saturday: Dress up and take selfies. Dress up and go for a promenade. Dress up and visit a gallery. Sunday: Get out all your old photo albums and take a trip down memory lane.
5.00 – 6.00 Supper	Nourishing hot meal
6.00 – 9.00 Relaxation	Watch a film Do a jigsaw Have a bath Read a book Listen to a podcast Sit in the garden and star gaze
9.00 – 10.00 Journal	Reflections on the day using the Elements as a structure Air: General contemplation – free writing Earth: What supported or nurtured you today? Fire: What actions or behaviours were important today? Water: A deeper reflection – insights, conclusions.

You Take It from Here – The Beauty Weave

At some point, you will want to create your own journaling path. The Beauty Weave is a simple way to begin.

Start by reflecting on some moments of beauty or truth that you have experienced in your life. This list will probably seem endless once you start working on it .... As you sit with the notion of beauty, recognise the sensations in your body – the thoughts and feelings as they occur – any images that might arise. Capture these moments in short phrases and write them as a list. When you have reached the bottom of your page, turn the paper 90 degrees and continue your list. You may want to use coloured pens – so the 'weave' that you create looks something like a loose weave cloth.

Use the Beauty Weave, one item each day, as the inspiration for a daily creative journaling practice.

I use the Beauty Weave to inspire a daily Haiku. Working with the Haiku structure (5 syllables, 7 syllables, 5 syllables) concentrates the attention and stops the mind from wandering whilst letting you gently slip into your honest and simple response to each beautiful moment of the day.

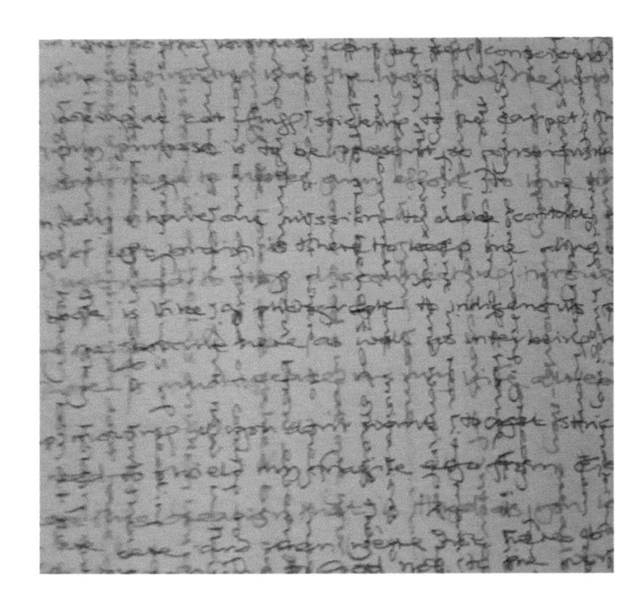

Here are some ideas for other ways in which you might want to explore your own creative journaling using the Beauty Weave or any other inspirations or themes that arise for you.

- Lists
- Word portraits
- Mind maps
- Unsent letters
- Imagined dialogue
- Straightforward description
- Free-writing
- Reflective writing
- Time lines or stepping stones
- Doodling, scribbling, free-style drawing
- Collage
- Making images with a variety of art materials (paint, inks, pastels, acrylics, crayon, pencil ...)
- Imagination – roaming freely through the imaginal realm
- Autobiography – factual or fictionalised
- Mandalas – getting to the heart of the matter, like a visual Haiku
- Writing poetry
- Choosing and prioritising
- Meditation, visualisation, contemplation
- Formulating and asking beautiful questions
- Taking a different perspective, zooming in or zooming out
- Dreams and Memories
- Turning points and milestones
- Map making
- Writing illegibly (useful for when you need to maintain privacy)
- Writing or drawing with your non-dominant hand
- Writing in straight lines. Writing in spirals or waves. Scatter gun words across the page.
- Experimenting with different kinds of writing utensils

Reflections

The beautiful questions in this section are intended to promote inspiration and contemplation. In addition, you may want to use the questions as journaling prompts and free write, doodle or create a masterpiece in response to them.

What has left a mark on your heart?

Would you like to be immortal?

How much do we shape our own lives? How much are they shaped by society?

'Is creativity just intelligence having fun?' (Albert Einstein)

Just as bees produce honey, what do you produce that brings sweetness to the world?

What do you have to say? (create your own profound and memorable quote)

When do you feel most real? Who or what brings you alive?

'The highest reward for a person's toil is not what they get for it, but what they become by it.' (John Ruskin) What are you becoming? How is your work shaping you?

Which fictional character would describe the very best of who you are? And the worst?

'Tell me what it is you plan to do with your one wild and precious life.' (Mary Oliver)

What fills you up? What depletes you?

What image represents the meaning of life for you?

How might an animal or plant experience the meaning of life?

What harsh truths do you prefer to ignore?

What will your future self remember about today?

Where does your sense of self worth come from?

Does hardship make us stronger? Does uncertainty build resilience?

What happens if you just let go? (of your self-image, stuff, space, relationships)

Who or what was your first love?

If life is a jigsaw puzzle – what piece would you be today?

What will you be harvesting from your life today?

Where is your true home?

What small pleasure from your childhood could you re-introduce into your life today?

Do you try to make reality mirror your dreams? Or do your dreams mirror reality?

Is there a small action you could perform to make someone's day?

What is delighting you right now?

What keeps you safe? Anchors and grounds you?

Who is the 'you' that has remained constant through all of the physical, emotional and intellectual transformations of your short life?

Are you driving your life or is it driving you?

What's the rush? What destination are you pelting towards?

Are you currently living in a state of sleep, creep or leap? (Stephanie Bennett Voigt)

'I would love to live like a river flows. Carried by the surprise of its own unfolding.' (John O'Donahue) Do you notice your own unfolding?

If you could re-live a moment from your life in slow motion – what would that moment be?

Where are the sticking points in your life? What are you putting off or avoiding?

If you could take one hour of your day to do whatever you liked, (no limits) what would you do?

Who do you seek approval from?

'How many roads must a man walk down, before they call him a man?' (Bob Dylan) What roads have you walked down?

How does your outlook colour your experiences? What if all humans focused on what is going right rather than on what is going wrong?

What does your spacesuit look like? Mindfulness teacher, Tara Brach, talks about how we hide our authentic vulnerable selves inside a protective space suit.

How brightly do you shine?

What is the main archetype or role that you play out in your life?

Who would you like to bump into today?

Who or what catapults you into presence?

What actions in your life have (or will have) the furthest reaching consequences?

In what ways do you short change yourself?

Can you let go of attachment to outcomes and just enjoy life as it emerges?

What will brighten your day when skies are grey?

Is there something you can do today that you've never tried before?

Where do you come from? Where are you rooted?

If all your dreams came true, how would that feel?

If you could travel to any moment in history – what would it be?

What does your pigeon-hole look like? How have you been stereo-typed?

What are your contributions to your community?

What could do with a good pruning or clear out in your life?

Are you creating enough space in your life for the things that you love?

Where are the ancestors? Can you spend some time with them?

What do you need help with right now? Can you ask for support?

'Do you write over what is already written?' (Rumi)

'Problems cannot be solved with the same mind set that created them.' (Albert Einstein) Can you apply this wisdom to your own difficulties?

To what do you attribute your success in life?

What kind of retreat would you love to have? (beach hut, tree house, cave, den...)

If you could live safely and happily with any exotic animal in its own natural habitat – what animal would it be?

If you are the sun and life is your radiance, how does your radiance manifest in this world?

What pledges can you make to support yourself? Others? The planet?

I sincerely hope that the prompts in this book have been helpful and that you will continue to have a regular and powerful journaling practice that nourishes the beautiful, wild being that you truly are.

Acknowledgements

I want to acknowledge some of the divine beings who have inspired love, beauty and truth in my life and who have shaped my way of thinking and being as I have written this book. I have mostly been influenced by poets, songwriters, philosophers, spiritual teachers, authors and ecologists who have been generous enough to eloquently share their truth with the world. Among them are:

Sharon Blackie – a psychologist, mythologist and ecologist. I have participated in several of her online courses and workshops, exploring the Mythic Imagination from an academic as well as an immersive point of view.

Tara Brach – psychologist, author and founder of the Insight Meditation Community of Washington DC. Tara is an internationally renowned mindfulness teacher and I have often found solace in her dharma talks and guided meditations (check out YouTube).

Julia Cameron – teacher, author, artist, poet, playwright, novelist, film maker, journalist, composer. Julia's devotion to the idea of creative recovery for everyone is exemplified by her own achievements. I know so many people for whom her book, The Artist's Way, has been a turning point.

Suzette Clough – psychotherapist, artist and teacher who developed Visual Medicine – a simple painting and writing process that is a conversation between human spirit and world, between what is known and what is emerging. I find the Visual Medicine process a template for how to live my daily life with an open heart and curiosity.

Leonard Cohen – singer/songwriter, poet and spiritual explorer.

Vivian Gladwell – Founder of Nose to Nose – a training organisation for improvisational theatre clowning. Over a period of five years training with Vivian I learned how not to be afraid – of others, of myself. From this I also learned how to love – others and myself.

Hafiz – Fourteenth century Persian poet.

Anne-Marie Jobin – a French Canadian teacher, author and art therapist who developed New Creative Journaling. Doing one of Anne-Marie's online courses propelled me from just writing in my journal to using a huge variety of creative expressions to investigate my days.

Anne Lamott – teacher, writer of fiction and non-fiction, public speaker. Her book, Bird by Bird – Instructions on Writing and Life, helped to free me from the constrictions of 'how it has always been done' and encouraged me to find my own way in writing.

Iain McGilchrist – Psychiatrist, writer and scholar. His book, The Master and His Emissary, gifted me the permission to value who I am, not who I thought I should be.

Jackie Morris – writer and illustrator. I don't know what to say about Jackie's work, except that it touches me so deeply. Her detailed drawings and paintings speak of stillness, silence, mystery, longing, connection, fulfilment – they spark a sense of possibility, they carry the scent of a happy ending.

Tracey Savage – artist. Her paintings are touching, imaginative, charming, eccentric, skillful, inspiring – all the things I love.

Mark Nepo – poet and spiritual adviser whose metaphors always take me straight to the heart of beauty.

Mary Oliver – Pulitzer Prize winning poet who wrote so many beautiful poems about the simple lessons we can learn from nature.

Rumi – Thirteenth century Persian poet and Sufi Mystic

Thich Nhat Hahn – Buddhist monk, teacher and peace activist. A gentle and wise soul.

Robin Wall Kimmerer – ecologist, Director of Centre for Native Peoples and the Environment, and author of several books including the wonderful Braiding Sweetgrass.

Kurt Vonnegutt – American writer – I find his dry sense of humour and existential take on life speaks to my own despair in a way that manages to lift me and re-instate some meaning.

David Whyte – Anglo-Irish poet who writes beautifully about the conversational nature of reality and takes us deeply into the human heart.

Special Thanks

I would like to offer special thanks to my dear friends, Michael Maynard and Carol Leader, for their spot-on questions, challenges and encouragement as this book evolved. Also thanks to my neighbour, Mike Gould, who brought a much needed fresh and objective eye to the manuscript. Finally, heart felt thanks to Anna Atkinson, my sometime partner in crime, who believed in me and encouraged me to put myself 'out there'.

About the Author

As a child, Jesus was my imaginary friend – I was a very good girl and did well at school. I was also self righteous and precocious. This didn't work out well for me and when I lost my Christian faith in my teen years I was filled with confusion which quickly turned to depression. Saved by a Guru, I lived a (much needed) tightly boundaried life in an ashram for a couple of years which gifted me a lifetime meditation practice.

My early career was in the theatre. I had devotedly attended Saturday matinees at the local rep theatre from the age of 8 through 18 and never lost the thrill of a live performance. My first job was in the box office, moving into Theatre Management and then working as part of the tiny team that opened The Actors Centre (London) and later at The Actors Institute (London).

When my kids came along, for pragmatic reasons, I moved into education, starting out as a lecturer– ending up as Head of Faculty in a large college of further and higher education. From the top of a very wobbly and increasingly beaurocrat ladder, I side-stepped into the criminal justice system - managing training and education programmes across several prisons and later facilitating group work interventions for the probation service. Alongside my work, I started to write morning pages, studied for a Masters Degree in Creative Writing and became involved in several Writing for Wellbeing networks.

When my children left home, I moved from England to Nepal to do voluntary work as a Management and Training Adviser with various NGOs for two years. My interest in Buddhism grew, my meditation practice deepened and, on my return home, I trained as a secular mindfulness teacher working mainly with Mental Health charities. Then, completely against the grain (I am basically an introvert), I spent five years training to be a clown. Contrary to all my pre-conceptions, clowning is about mindful relationship, listening, being open, being kind, being courageous. The red nose is the smallest mask – so clowning is very much about making the authentic self visible.

I am currently training to be a Death Doula with the organisation Living Well Dying Well, and have been a volunteer at a local hospice for several years. I see the main purpose of creative journaling to be a support in ensuring a life well lived each and every day.

My most recent influences have been New Creative Journaling (Anne Marie Jobin) and an exploration of the Mythic Imagination (Sharon Blackie). Both of these, very different, approaches freed up and strengthened my own imaginal world in the most delightful ways and led to me writing a daily page on Facebook – Beyond Words – which evolved into this book.

Beyond Words has brought together all of my Gods into one temple. Spirituality, creativity, domesticity, psychology, philosophy, wellbeing, imagination, love of nature and just a touch of magic.

PRINTED AND BOUND BY:
Copytech (UK) Limited trading as Printondemand-worldwide,
9 Culley Court, Bakewell Road, Orton Southgate.
Peterborough, PE2 6XD, United Kingdom.